Let Your He

Spirituality for Contemplatives in Action

Michael J Cunningham SDB

DON BOSCO

Credits

© Don Bosco Publications 2009
Thornleigh House Sharples Park
BOLTON BL1 6PQ Phone 01204 308811
Email joyce@salesians.org.uk
www.don-bosco-publications.co.uk

Photos
Front Cover - Jim Clough

ISBN 978-0-9555654-2-7

Contents

Foreword

The world is constantly flashing images before us, enticing us to find happiness in many ways – being the right size, having good looks, being successful in business, using the best techniques to communicate, being the perfect family, putting me at the centre of my universe. In other words, all the factors that can make us achieve the so-called *A list* in life.

In *Let Your Heart Pray*, Michael shows us the path to true happiness and to finding the real *A list* of life. He reminds us that none of us is perfect and that we don't live in a perfect world. As he puts it, we need the container (the external, the without) and the contents (the internal, the within). Both are essential for our spiritual journey. I particularly liked his use of the labyrinth to explain the inner and outer dimensions of our quest, reinforcing how the inner and outer lives are profoundly connected.

In our spiritual journey we look for writers who will say it *as it is*, who make the journey clearer. We look for writers with whom we can identify, who speak our language, who understand the lights and shadows that make up our lives. Such a writer is Michael. He challenges us when he speaks of the world we have known as never returning, that we are on a new path and that change is at the heart of the journey we are making. He develops his thoughts about contemplation – the long loving look at reality, seeing with the eye of the heart. He gives a very clear introduction to Centering Prayer.

Throughout the book, Michael then weaves various threads with which we can relate so well. He talks of God's unconditional love, forgiveness, compassion and mercy. He deals with pain, with our fears, knowing our true selves, silence and stillness. He speaks of imagining oneself sitting by the river and letting each distraction be like a boat floating down. *Name it, identify it and gently let it go*, he says. Sometimes it can seem as if it is peak hour traffic going down that river! To me, however, Michael gives the ways in which we can deal with all these threads and not take our eye off the core – that only love can know God.

No matter what our calling in life, if we want a book that lifts us up, that consoles, that gives hope, that recognizes our humanness, that speaks to us and draws us closer to God, that encourages us to journey on the greatest adventure of all, then this is the book! While *Let Your Heart Pray* stands alone, I would also strongly recommend Michael's previous books. To me, one of the signs of a good spiritual book is the impact it has on my life when I put the book down and live out my day. With Michael's writings I find myself relating his themes to the practicalities of my life, be it in prayer or action.

Contemplative prayer is a gift from God. Michael's *Let Your Heart Pray* is another gift from God.

Sister Mary Monaghan

Superior General

Sisters of Nazareth

Chapter One

A New World

It is our vision of reality that is undergoing a
monumental change in our present time, causing
us to perceive and understand ourselves in our
relationships – to other people, to our planet and to
the Transcendent – in an entirely new way.[1]

[1] Adrian B Smith *A Reason for Living & Hoping* (St Pauls Publishing London 2002) p 19

The world we have known will never return. We are on a new path and change is at the heart of the journey. Some have argued that the destruction of the Twin Towers in New York is the symbol that things will never be the same again. That may be true, but in itself, that shocking event which was probably viewed on television screens all over the world, marked the culmination of a century of wars, of increasing violence, torture and genocide, revolutions and social upheavals; sadly this madness may not be ended. Today we face the threat of international terrorism, driven by a fanatical extremism that simply wishes to destroy innocent life. Sadly, much of this extremism is fuelled by religious fundamentalism, which distorts what is meant to bring peace and harmony to the world and turns it into poison. Religious culture has traditionally praised and honoured martyrs for the faith; today we shake our heads in despair at the indiscriminate destruction by the suicide bomber. We even see children exploited and brainwashed into becoming human bomb-carriers. These facts suggest that our world is becoming dangerously fragmented.

I think that this fragmentation is a deeply misguided response to profound changes that are happening in our times. We may be reaching a point in history that anthropologists are calling an axial period. The term was coined by the philosopher Karl Jaspers to refer to what he called a paradigm shift in human history. A paradigm describes our customary way of looking at and thinking about reality. Such profound change is immensely challenging to how we think and feel about ourselves and our destiny. The rise of fundamentalism is a symptom of many who cannot cope with what is happening. It also points to concern about the injustices in our world, the great discrepancies in wealth and use of resources. Rather than deal with this reality and work to create a better world, the fundamentalists choose to destroy and to kill.

At the heart of the paradigm shift, which we are experiencing today, lies the replacement of the Newtonian world-view, which regarded the world as a set of building blocks, fixed objects, operating to unchanging laws. Such a world-view relied on predictability and clear distinctions between solid objects. Newton's view has been replaced with Quantum Theory, which was developed in the 1920s and it has opened up an unseen world of sub-atomic neutrons, protons and electrons. Far from being a world of clear boundaries and distinctions, the quantum world reveals that everything – and therefore everybody – is deeply related and connected. It seems that far from being stable and predictable; reality is governed by uncertainty and probability. But it is deeply connected.

This deep connection is rooted in the basic structure of the universe. All the potentials and possibilities for life were present in that first trillionth of a trillionth of a second of the Big Bang which scientists tell us occurred 13.7 billion years ago. If that moment had happened one trillionth of a trillionth of a percent slower, the universe would have imploded. If it had occurred one trillionth of a trillionth of a percent faster, matter would have been forced apart in such a way that nothing would have been shaped and formed. The Hubble telescope has revealed that our universe is still expanding and includes not just our galaxy but billions of galaxies and billions of stars. What is apparent is not just the size and grandeur of the universe, but the extraordinary intelligence and deep mystery, at the heart of it, as a guiding presence. To gaze at the stars is to look back at our origins and to see our future shaped by the intelligence of our Creator. The fact that we can be *conscious* of this unfolding mystery, as we shall see later in the book, is of immense importance in the understanding of a contemporary spirituality.

Although there are powerful forces at work trying to fragment and divide our world, scientists are revealing the essential unity manifested in all created things. All life shares the same basic cells. We seem to have two opposing forces at work in our times. Those who wish to keep the world divided, and those who wish to reveal and celebrate its underlying unity. One of the most dramatic signs is the whole area of ecological awareness. To many, this appears quite new but it is in fact a recovery of a spiritual insight which the medievals called the Great Chain of Being, which saw all things as part of a greater whole. It rests on the conviction that our planet and its eco-systems are deeply connected. Concerns about destruction of the environment and global-warming are in the background to all political decisions these days. It would be better if they were in the foreground; but the awareness of the importance of this issue reminds us that we are not masters of the world as we recently thought, but that we hold this planet in trust for future generations.

How we respond to the new world of deep connection and relationship is crucial for the future of our planet. Scientists today are tending to use the kind of language that mystics had intuited centuries ago. One of the most dramatic events of recent years was the exploration of space by man. The astronauts had a unique and totally novel view of planet earth and its place in the cosmos. Here are some examples of their reactions to what they saw and experienced:[2]

> I love looking on the Earth. It isn't important whose she is, just that she is. *Oleg At'kov (USSR)*

---

[2] Quoted in *Reclaiming Spirituality* Diarmuid O'Murchu (Gill & Macmillan Dublin 1997) p 44-45

Seeing the Earth for the first time, I could not help but love and cherish her. *Taylor Wang (China)*

On the return trip home, gazing through 240,000 miles of space towards the stars and planet from which I had come, I suddenly experienced the universe as intelligent, loving and harmonious. My view of the planet was a glimpse of divinity. *Edgar Mitchell (USA)*

You realise that on that small spot, that little blue and white thing is everything that means anything to you – all of history and music, and poetry and art and death and birth and love, tears, joy, games, all of it on that little spot out there. You recognise that you are part of that total life. *Russell Schweikart (USA)*

Anyone interested in spirituality will be fascinated by the language used by these astronauts of different nationalities and cultures. There are many similarities with the contemplative and mystical tradition. The Russian, At'kov, speaks of *looking* at the earth. Contemplation has been described as *a long loving look at reality*. It is, as we shall see, more about looking rather than judging and critiquing. His looking moves him beyond possession and ownership to celebrating the fact *that she is*. The same reaction is provoked in the Chinese astronaut, Taylor Wang, whose gazing at the Earth moves him to love and cherish her. The American, Edgar Mitchell, experiences the Universe as intelligent and loving. He has a glimpse of divinity. The remarks by Russell Schweikart are in a similar vein as he sees the totality of all that the Earth contains, with a real sense of underlying unity. He then goes on to make this significant comment:

When you come back there is a difference in that world now. There is a difference in that relationship between you and that planet and you and all those other forms of life on that planet, *because you have had that kind of experience.*[3]

This is a crucial insight in understanding the nature of spirituality in our times. It is rooted in experience. These astronauts had a unique experience and their whole world-view was radically altered. They had glimpsed the underlying unity at the heart of the universe and the beauty and fragility of planet earth. The divisions and conflicts that often disfigure human existence were transformed into an experience of the harmony at the heart of all reality.

---

[3] Author's italics

It is this longing and hunger for beauty and harmony, for a sense of the bigger picture, that is driving the contemporary search for a more meaningful spirituality in our world today. There is a shift between the externals of rules, doctrines, authority structures and rituals, what might be called the outer structure of religion, to the inner and more spontaneous experience of spirituality. The Franciscan priest, Richard Rohr, calls this the distinction between the container and the contents. Since the time of the Reformation, there has been great emphasis on the container element of religion, to the detriment of the inner life of experience. Over-concentration on the externals of religion creates a false emphasis on law, and obedience to authority, on boundaries and questions as to who is in and who is not. If, on the other hand, all these externals are ignored and jettisoned, then the spiritual searcher faces a very lonely path, which can become very dangerous and egocentric without any kind of guidance and account-ability. Healthy growth is based on *both/and* rather than *either/or*. We need both, but there is no doubt that the desire and search for inner experience is becoming a crucial sign of our times. This can create tensions with religious authority but it is a sign of the growing spiritual maturity which the Holy Spirit is prompting and creating in response to the hungers of our age. We need a healthy spirituality that can find a more creative relationship to both the inner and outer world.

The renewed search for an inner and more meaningful life is not just a response to the over emphasis on religious externals by institutional religion, but also to the cultural climate of postmodernism which seeks to deny the soul's search for meaning. After the Reformation, the Enlightenment attempted to sideline God and put man firmly at the centre of all things. Reason was enthroned in the place of faith. Liberation from religious shackles would bring about the secular utopia. We have all seen the amazing benefits of science and technology, but this has come at a very high price. While producing so many improvements to our lives, reason alone could not save us from ourselves. The twentieth century became the century of world wars, of the holocaust, of genocide, and of ethnic cleansing. Sadly, the same pattern of violence is continuing in the twenty-first century, with the added threat of fundamentalist-inspired international terrorism.

Our postmodern culture has brought some benefits such as the liberation of minorities suppressed by racial, gender and sexual discrimination. But the overall impact of postmodernism has been deconstruction rather than construction. We are left with a world in which I have been liberated, but with no sense of meaning other than what I choose for myself. Choice extends not just to what

I can buy but also to my values which have no common grounding in objective truth. We are in a pic'n'mix world where everything is up for grabs and nothing is of any great value.

We find ourselves living on a conveyor belt of consumer goods which are constantly changing and being updated. Image is more important than what lies beneath. Institutions, which in the past would have provided stability and guidance, have been deconstructed and we are left with a deeply cynical view of the world. Even the humour of today takes a mocking form as significant figures are reduced to figures of fun and derision. This is not a healthy world and it abandons individuals to create meaning for themselves. It is a very heavy burden and we see so much addictive and angry behaviour as a consequence.

Human beings cannot live without meaning and it is capitalism which has taken over the values-vacuum created by postmodernism. *I shop therefore, I am* has become the new religious mantra. While attempting to liberate minorities, postmodernism has been helpless in liberating the poor, the outsider, the asylum seeker, the refugee: all victims of the new world order. This is where the new interest in spirituality is truly challenged. The inner search for meaning and transcendence has to be accompanied by an equal commitment to the poor and to social justice. No one articulated this message more strongly than the Hebrew prophets, and the essential link between the inner and outer life was brilliantly put together by Jesus in two great one-liners in the gospel – *The Father and I are One and Whatever you do to the least of these brothers and sisters of mine, you do to me.*[4]

Jesus here reveals the true nature of all religion and spirituality: making two into one. Where postmodernism abandons us to a rootless world without meaning, spirituality reveals that the significance of our lives is given to us by a transcendent God. We are led out of the despair of postmodern individualism into the security of an unconditional love and compassion. This is intuitively understood by the mother who comforts her crying child at night with the words, *It's OK.* She might not be able to explain that rationally, but at the level of heart and soul she knows it to be true. This is a sign of the inner wisdom that mystics and theologians tell us is the indwelling of God at the very core of our being. The same conviction motivates the volunteer and the missionary to work for the protection of the poor of the world and the victims of its violence.

What we are seeing today is the coming together of the two essential journeys of the spiritual life; the journey without and the journey within, the marriage of

---

inner and outer, of Mary and Martha, as we strive to create a new world built on the essential unity of all things and all people.

At the heart of this new interest in the inner life is the recovery of a tradition that had largely become lost in the Christian Churches – the tradition of contemplative prayer, which I shall explore in this book. Authentic contemplative prayer does not take us out of this world. In fact the opposite should be the case. Authentic prayer leads to authentic action, as we strive to put our relationship with God and our relationship with those in need on the same level as Jesus did. We need to integrate the vision and practice of the Hebrew prophets and the Christian mystics.

One of the encouraging signs of this is the new openness and respect for other religious traditions. Traditionally the West has favoured action over prayer and reflection, while eastern religions have favoured the inner life over the outer one. This was dramatically represented in the meeting of two of the giants of contemporary spirituality, the Cistercian monk, Thomas Merton, and the Buddhist monk, Thich Nhat Hanh. After the meeting, both men described each other as brothers. What they have given to the world is a new kind of spirituality, which is best described as *engaged spirituality*. It takes seriously the need to practise contemplative prayer and to live out that practice in a spirituality of non-violent living in a violent world. It is a spirituality of peace in a world of war, of compassion instead of indifference, of joy despite a world of suffering, of openness to *the Other* rather than rejection, a spirituality of love rather than fear. It is a spirituality that includes rather than excludes.

It is a different way of seeing and different way of being in the world. It recognises the fundamental unity of all things. It is not an easy spirituality, but one that engages with the ego, both at individual and collective levels, and this is far from easy. It looks for spiritual transformation, rather than religion as a belonging system in which I can feel good about myself, while endlessly judging others. It moves beyond worthiness to a recognition that we are not in control of our spiritual lives. Our spiritual practice of contemplative prayer will soon bring us up against our essential poverty and vulnerability before God. That is why many will not walk this difficult path, that the anonymous 14th century author famously called *The Cloud of Unknowing*. It moves us beyond the calculating, judgemental mind of everyday thinking, to a compassion that embraces and accepts everything. The work for social justice, therefore, is not rooted in anger, but in understanding and wisdom that recognises that I too am part of the evil that I see in others. The essential insight, at the heart of all this, is that I cannot transform myself. The work of transformation is the work of the Holy Spirit. It is not striving to become a better person, but becoming a new creation. This is a gift of grace, and all we have to do is to receive it.

Some of our scientists are confirming what the mystics always told us: that life is a mystery that we cannot control. We cannot control it with our egos and our dominative patterns of behaviour; we have to surrender to it. What this means is learning to become present to the gift of Being which surrounds us at every moment of our lives and is always available to us. Presence to the mystery of love is rooted in consciousness and awareness. All great spiritual teachers have taught the wisdom of awareness. It turns theology into poetry. It is learning to look at and to receive what is real in a loving contemplative gaze rather than the judgemental, analytical mind that seeks to create distance between me and *the Other*. It is learning to say *Yes* before we say *No*.

Included in this compassionate acceptance is a willingness to own and acknowledge my own imperfections and see them not just as obstacles in my spiritual journey, but as the very means that will lead me to meet the compassionate, forgiving lover that is God. Once I can include my own brokenness, I can reach out to the brokenness of others and to the brokenness of the world, with a healing touch that truly reconciles differences and brings all of us into the unity which is the Body of Christ.

Our western minds teach us to build a better world by changing others. The contemplative mind teaches us that we change the world by changing ourselves.

Chapter Two
Recovering a Lost Tradition

The interconnectedness and interdependence
of everything that exists is the way the scientific
community is beginning to understand material
reality. Most of us have yet to be convinced of this
basic structure of the universe. The most effective
way to grasp this truth is to experience it. This
is one of the precious gifts that the discipline of
Contemplative prayer communicates.[5]

---

[5] Thomas Keating *Manifesting God* (Lantern Books New York 2005) p 7

Having experienced the wonder of space travel, Astronaut Russell Schweikart returned to Earth a different man. Like his fellow astronauts, his perspective had been radically altered by his new experience. He now looked at everything differently. In the above quotation, Thomas Keating suggests that the same is true for spirituality. If we are to live and survive in the twenty-first century, we need to see the essential unity that holds all things together; the unity at the heart of all reality. Contemplation is an experience of a realised union with God. Once it has been experienced, everything changes. This insight has profound and very practical consequences for our times and for all our relationships: to ourselves, to others and to the created world. Without this perspective, our world will continue to fragment and ever more dangerous conflicts will break out. The hijackers, who destroyed the World Trade Center in New York, turned western technology against itself by flying planes into the Twin Towers. We remain threatened by the possible use of chemical and biological warfare, with frightening consequences. The people who died in the Twin Towers had simply gone to work, when they met their totally unexpected and violent deaths. The world has indeed changed after centuries when only soldiers died in battle.

When the Cistercian monk Thomas Merton got permission from his superiors to travel to the East in 1968, he went in search of eastern ways of prayer and contemplation. Shortly before his untimely death, he wrote a letter back to his monastery, at Gethsemane in Kentucky, and told them that everything he had discovered in his eastern journey already existed in the western Christian tradition. The problem was that it had been largely forgotten. Merton, in fact, was not initially popular in his own monastery because he told the Cistercians, perhaps the strictest religious order in the Catholic Church, that they were not really contemplatives. He accused them of simply *saying prayers*, and saying prayers is not the same as praying contemplatively. Contemplative prayer is beyond words, thoughts, images and emotions.

There have always been two traditions of prayer in the Christian Church: vocal prayer such as saying prayers, and non-vocal prayer, which is the contemplative tradition. Both go back to Jesus. Sadly, in the last four hundred years or so, the non-vocal type of contemplative prayer had almost disappeared in the Church. The Reformation was particularly damaging to the contemplative tradition; it was a time when oppositional thinking took over and split Christianity. Reality was seen as black or white, either/or, right or wrong. There was no room for ambiguity and none for mystery. All that mattered was who had the right formulas and doctrines. The fact that love was the basis of Christianity was completely lost, as Catholics and Protestants tortured and brutally killed each other, in the name of Christ! This was dualistic thinking, at its worst and most dangerous. The contemplative vision that sees everything as fundamentally united was sidelined and almost forgotten. It is only re-emerging in our time.

The Enlightenment further reinforced this shift to left-brained thinking. *I think therefore I am* declared Descartes, as he reduced human wisdom and knowledge to the human mind. Here again, the human brain alone cannot deal with the mystery at the heart of all reality, with ambiguity, with paradox, with the complexity of things and of people. We cannot approach spiritual realities with the same mind that we use to get through our everyday work. We will never see the bigger picture, because we will simply try to fit everything into our normal way of looking at things. Most of us find it very difficult to move out of our comfort-zones. The realm of politics illustrates this very clearly. Left and right, liberal and conservative, look at a situation and interpret it from their own valid, but narrow, perspective. Only the contemplative mind can see the truth in both positions and bring about a richer, deeper perspective that can include what appear to be polar opposites and go beyond them. This is true seeing. It is exactly what many Christians in the Reformation were unable to do. Today, our politicians and some religious leaders are caught in the same straightjacket. It is reduced to winners and losers, good guys and bad guys. In contrast, the contemplative mind creates a space big enough so that all can be winners.

Now it is obviously a good thing to say prayers, but the Church seemed to have forgotten the specific instruction of Jesus in Matthew's gospel:

> Whenever you pray, go into your room and shut the door, pray to your Father in secret; and your Father who sees in secret will reward you.[6]

Jesus is not speaking about vocal prayer here. He is referring to wordless prayer, in the secret of the heart or the soul. He indicates clearly that the Father is already dwelling in the centre of our souls. He also stresses that we do not need many words when praying like this:

> When you are praying, do not heap up empty phrases as the Gentiles do; for they think that they will be heard because of their many words. Do not be like them, for your Father knows what you need before you ask him.[7]

---

[6] Mt 6:6
[7] Mt 6:7-8

The contemplative tradition rests on the wonderful reality of the divine indwelling. Immediately we are brought up against the mystery of God and his presence to all things and in all things. This is not something we can earn. It is not an achievement of human willpower. It is all about loving presence, a loving awareness of the mystery of Being that is God, a way of seeing reality as it truly is. Our minds can only take us so far on this road; they will never comprehend the mystery of God. Great mystics, like St Augustine and St John of the Cross, and countless others, make this very clear. The mind can never comprehend God; only love can know God. That is why contemplative prayer may be impossible for a Doctor of Philosophy, who is full of egoism, but perfectly easy for uneducated but very loving people.

What Jesus says about this kind of prayer comes from his felt experience. This is the way he prayed. Our normal image of Jesus is of someone constantly responding to the needs of others. We sometimes miss the fact that he was prepared to send people away so he could have time to re-connect with that inner relationship of intimacy that he had with his Father:

> Immediately he made the disciples get into the boat and go on ahead to the other side, while he dismissed the crowds. And after he had dismissed the crowds he went up the mountain by himself to pray.[8]

When Jesus invites us to go into our room and pray in secret, he is inviting us to share the very same relationship of intimacy and union that he had with his Father. That statement might seem almost shocking but Jesus doesn't hold back. In that wonderful prayer of Jesus, in John 14, he constantly uses the language of union and of intimacy when speaking of how close God is to us, closer in fact than we are to ourselves. When he asks the Father to send the Holy Spirit he tells us that the Spirit is dwelling within us:

> You know him because he abides with you he will be in you.[9]

> On that day you will understand that I am in the Father and you in me and I in you.[10]

> Those who love me will keep my word, and my Father will love them, and we will come to them and make our home with them.[11]

---

[8] Mt 14:22-23
[9] Jn 14:17
[10] v 20
[11] v 23

This kind of intimacy is pure gift. All we have to do is humbly receive it. Contemplative prayer is never a question of searching for God, although we often speak about the spiritual search. We already possess what we are looking for: the God within. Nevertheless we can speak meaningfully about the spiritual journey – and there is clear evidence for this in the Bible – as long as we remember that what we will discover is a place we have always known, however dimly. Poets understand the paradoxes at the heart of all authentic spirituality. The oft-quoted lines of T S Eliot spring to mind:

> We shall not cease from exploration
> And the end of our exploring
> Will be to arrive where we started
> And know the place for the first time.[12]

We will have changed as we undergo the paschal experience of death to the ego, which may take many years, and then we can begin to see in a new way. We will see what previously we have been unable to see, and to experience what we have been unable to experience. This is sharing in the new life of the Risen Christ. Recently, while preaching retreats in the United States, I met a missionary who had spent thirty years working in Africa. He told me that when some tribal people make a fire they cover it with mud. The fire beneath can barely be seen or felt. In many ways that image sums up our normal levels of awareness with respect to the divine indwelling. It is always there within but we live our lives oblivious to this amazing reality. St Theresa of Avila used to say that most of us pray to an absent God.

The teaching of Jesus about wordless prayer, of learning to quieten our active lives and be still, is not just found in the New Testament. For some years now I have been involved in work to support asylum seekers and refugees here in Liverpool where I live. As a Salesian priest, I try to connect this work with young people. When I visit schools, I usually take the Bible with me and hold it open at the very first page where we read these words:

> God created humankind in his image, in the image of God he
> created them, male and female he created them.[13]

Right from the very beginning of the Judaeo-Christian scriptures, we are described, at our very origins, as carrying within us the image of God in our

---

[12] T S Eliot *Four Quartets* (Faber and Faber London 1959) p 48
[13] Gen 1:27

souls. This applies to every single person on this planet. It applies to the people we like and the people we don't like, to our friends as to our enemies. It applies to those who wish us well and also to the terrorist who might wish to kill us.

Mature religion and spirituality should lead us beyond the kind of dualism that dominates our ordinary ways of thinking. The Jewish people struggled with this very radical teaching, as we all do. There is the danger of thinking that God likes good people (like us) and dislikes bad people (like them). Every human group, religious or otherwise, plays this dualistic game – dividing people into good guys, that God will reward, and bad guys, that God will punish. Our group is made in the image and likeness of God, that group is not. I would suggest that the majority of church-going Christians who wouldn't dream of missing church on a Sunday will think this way.

And this is the problem. It is perfectly possible to say prayers, to attend church, to go to Mass, fulfil one's duties, and still keep our lives ego-centred. Spirituality should move us from an ego-centred life to the discovery of *the true self* which lies hidden beneath the ego. The insights of modern psychology demonstrate how we all need our egos for protection in the early years of our lives. Our parents try to love us unconditionally, but sooner or later they start to tell us that we must behave properly and perform well to win that love. This does great damage to the vulnerable child who starts to believe that he or she is only worthy of love if it is earned by good behaviour. We then fall into the trap of *the performance principle*. We no longer feel loved and valued because of who we are, but because of what we do. The ego sets out to protect this vulnerability with a series of games to provide security and protection. We move from our *Being* mode to our *Doing* mode.

The problem is that our deeper and truer self is based on being not doing. It tries to break through the shell of the ego, from time to time, by hinting at and providing insights into the wider reality of being. We experience the sheer beauty of being when looking at a beautiful sunset, or walking by the ocean or in the hills, or looking at the face of a child or a loved one, or sharing the gift of friendship, or reading a poem or looking at a work of art. At these moments the mud over the fire in our souls is disturbed and we catch a glimpse of the fire and the glory within. This is precisely what happened with those astronauts in space who found their normal way of looking at reality changed. They saw the underlying beauty in all things. It was a break-through of mystical experience when they saw reality as it truly is. This sense of a different self is what the mystics speak about and is available to us when we go into our inner room and connect with the reality of God within. It is not an extraordinary moment; if we practise contemplative prayer it becomes our normal way of seeing.

In recent years, I have preached retreats in many parts of the world and I am convinced that the Holy Spirit is speaking to many people, religious and lay, at this deeper dimension of being. I think this is happening in response to the cultural desert, that we are living in, which denies any significant meaning to our human activity. I also think that this tradition is being rediscovered in the Christian Churches because for too long we have looked at religion through exclusively rational eyes. Mystics of all religions suggest that reality has many levels and we need a new way of uncovering these different levels of consciousness and awareness beyond the rational. We are learning to connect the left brain of reason, logic and analysis with the right brain of intuition, symbolism, art, poetry, paradox and wisdom.

The new world of quantum physics is supporting this more complex view of reality. Scientists have put on a new humility, as they constantly reveal the mystery that surrounds us at every moment and in every corner of the universe. They have become more comfortable with paradox than many religious leaders. The more we discover, the less we know. Physics speaks of light behaving like a particle and at the same time like a wave. Both are true at the same time, contradicting the rational logic of western philosophy. The mystic would have no trouble with such a paradox, and clearly, neither would Jesus. He used parables not logic, to describe the new reality of God's presence in the world which he called the Kingdom of God. For Jesus, the last shall be first, the poor are rich, the rich are poor, strength is weakness, weakness is strength, and even death is life.

I have suggested that the world, which we are experiencing these days, is on the cusp of a quite dramatic change. Men and women of wisdom and insight, from all religions are telling us that we are experiencing a revolution of consciousness, which will profoundly affect how we think and feel about ourselves. Essentially this is change at the level of spiritual awareness and it centres on the realisation that everything is connected, that everything and everyone is related, at the level of being. This is calling for a recovery of contemplative consciousness which will release a new creativity in the human spirit. It will enable us to find the energy and the drive to make real the vision articulated by Jesus, when he spoke about the divine indwelling and the divine life that is in all of us. This is our most personal energy and identity. It reveals the relational drive that is at the heart of the universe. The writer of the letter to the Ephesians understood this vision:

He has let us know the mystery of his purpose, the hidden plan he so kindly made in Christ from the beginning, to act upon when the times had run their course to the end: that he would bring everything together under Christ, as head, everything in the heavens and everything on earth.[14]

If we all share this gift that we are all made in the image of God, then divisions, conflict and wars no longer make sense.

The message of the gospel is so radical that it takes us a long time to understand it. God seems to be very patient with us. Just think how long it took to abolish slavery, to give freedom and equality to women, to recognise the dignity of the disabled. These are still ongoing projects. If we are to respond to the challenges of our time, we need a new way of seeing, a new consciousness. This will bring about a new sense of unity, the gift of wisdom and compassion, the recovery of what has been called *the sacred feminine*. Perhaps we can understand what that great twentieth century theologian, Karl Rahner, meant when he said that the Christian of the future will either become a mystic or cease to exist. We are not talking about a five-year plan here, but a movement for change which is only just beginning and will stretch long into the future. It can be called the Long Spiritual Revolution.

When we speak of revolution, we do not mean something like a mere *coup d'etat* whereby one set of rulers is replaced by another set while the structure of ruling itself remains basically the same – that is only a rebellion. A genuine revolution must be a *gestalt shift* in the whole way of seeing our relations to one another so that our behaviour patterns are reformed from the inside out. Any revolution worthy of the name must be primarily a revolution in consciousness.[15]

I agree with Beatrice Bruteau in situating this revolution at the level of consciousness. Political and social revolutions throughout history tend to bring about change from the top. New structures are put in place, the past is usually ignored and forgotten and yet within a few years little has changed. Many idealistic movements, such as the French revolution or the Communist revolution, began in hope and ended in the same old violence and repression of dissidents. A reactionary ego or a revolutionary ego is still an ego.

---

[14] Eph 1:8-1
[15] Beatrice Bruteau *The Grand Option* (University of Notre Dame Press Indiana 2001) p 17

For real change to take place there has to be a recognition of self-critical thinking, as the Hebrew prophets made clear. We have to find a way to own our dark side, our shadow. This cannot happen without some inner work, which enables us to confront the essential flaws in the human condition, that everybody experiences. Counselling and psychology can help here but nothing goes as deep as prayer which is the means that God has given us for the deepest kind of healing – and it is entirely free and available every day of our lives.

Fortunately, in our times, the Holy Spirit is prompting a rediscovery of the contemplative tradition of wordless prayer. Following the ground-breaking work of Thomas Merton many great spiritual teachers are now introducing more and more people to this wonderful gift. There are centres such as Contemplative Outreach[16] led by Thomas Keating and Basil Pennington. There is the Center for Action and Contemplation in Alberquerque, New Mexico,[17] led by Richard Rohr. There is the World Meditation Movement,[18] led by John Main and Laurence Freeman, among others. There are teachers such as Cynthia Bourgeault, James Finlay and Ruth Burrows. The invitation from Jesus is clear and direct:

> Ask, and it will be given to you; search, and you will find; knock, and the door will opened for you. For everyone who asks receives, and everyone who searches finds, and for everyone who knocks, the door will be opened.[19]

---

[16] www.centeringprayer.com
[17] www.caradicalgrace.com
[18] www.wccm.org
[19] Mt 7:7-9

Chapter Three
The Practice of Contemplative Prayer

I have no programme for this seeing. It is only
given. But the gate of heaven is everywhere.[20]

---

[20] Thomas Merton *Conjectures of a Guilty Bystander* (Image Books Doubleday NY1968) p 158

One conviction that all religions and religious teachers share is that we need different eyes to see spiritual reality. If we simply continue to look with the everyday eyes of the calculating mind our vision will always remain limited and superficial. To open ourselves to the great mysteries of love and truth, suffering and pain, we need a new way of seeing that is rooted in a different kind of experience. We all tend to filter reality to fit our own preferred way of seeing things, our comfort-zones. Postmodern culture reinforces that filtering grid by trapping us at the surface of things in the endless fascination with sensory experience, with constant entertainment and celebrity gossip. In contrast, mature religion has always pointed to the necessity of some kind of silence, of deep prayer, of meditation to gain access to the deeper realities of our souls. The normal mind of everyday awareness remains profoundly dualistic, and reads everything in terms of either/or, black or white, good or bad. It has to divide the field. Such a mind cannot deal with mystery and ambiguity. It tends to reinforce the divided and fragmented atmosphere that we live in today as we close ourselves off to the stranger, the foreigner, the person who is different. We strive to build higher walls to reinforce our defensive strategy in what we see as an ever-threatening world. It is not surprising that an increasing number of people are showing interest in what I called in the last chapter *The Long Spiritual Revolution*. At the heart of this revolution is the recovery of the contemplative tradition that shuts out the clamour and noise of contemporary life and invites us into the silence of our deepest selves. We are trying to recover our souls.

For too long this tradition has been closed off to the ordinary person, even to many professionally religious people, such as priests and religious. Contemplation was seen as a rather esoteric practice for the chosen few who might be that way inclined, spiritual introverts who had little interest, and still less impact, on the way things are in the modern world. Many regular churchgoers remain largely ignorant of this tradition and its riches. But an increasing number are singing a new song. I have always been impressed with the life of Cardinal Joseph Bernadin of Chicago, a friend of Cardinal Basil Hume. Bernadin describes a moment in his life when he became more fully aware of the promptings of the God within him. Even though he was living a good and apostolic life in the Church he felt a restlessness inside himself:

> I came to understand that the pace of my life and the direction of
> my activity were unfocused, uncentered in a significant way. This
> created a certain unrest. I came to realize that I needed to make
> some changes in my life, and chief among these was a renewal of

personal prayer. Mention of prayer may evoke an image of *saying* prayers, of reciting formulas. I mean something quite different. When we speak of the renewal of prayer in our lives, we are speaking of reconnecting ourselves with the larger mystery of life and of our common existence. This implies becoming disciplined in the use of our time, in the use of Centering Prayer, and in the development of a contemplative stance towards life. When this happens, we begin to experience healing, integration, wholeness, peacefulness. We begin to hear more clearly the echoes of the Word in our own lives, in our own hearts. And as that Word takes root in the depths of our being, it begins to grow and to transform the way we live. It affects our relationships with people around us and above all our relationship with the Lord. From this rootedness flow our energies, our ministry, our ways of loving. From this core we can proclaim the Lord Jesus and his Gospel not only with faith and conviction but also with love and compassion.[21]

In this account Bernadin describes how the Spirit spoke to him in the depths of his being as he was experiencing the restlessness of an unfocused and very busy life, and how he introduced the discipline of regular practice of what he called Centering Prayer. He describes the changes this brought about in his life as the gifts of the Spirit became more evident. He experienced integration and healing, discovering that his teaching and practice of the faith became more compassionate and understanding. His relationships to people and to God underwent transformation. This growth in the gifts of the Holy Spirit and a deepening of the sense of compassion are clear signs of transformation.

I was touched when I read these words because they echoed a similar experience I had in my own priestly ministry. I was preaching a Retreat to Salesian Sisters in Newark, New Jersey some years ago and was sitting before the Blessed Sacrament during evening exposition. I became aware that The Holy Spirit within me was calling me to a deeper level of intimacy in my life, especially prayer life. A few days after the Retreat I was staying in our Salesian parish in the Lower East Side of New York City. In the library I found a copy of *Intimacy with God* by Thomas Keating. I devoured the book in one sitting and later bought a copy for myself. This book introduced me to the practice of Centering Prayer which Benardin also referred to. Since then, I have tried to remain faithful to the daily practice of Centering Prayer.

---

[21] Quoted in *Centred Living* Basil Pennington (Redemptorist Publications UK 1999) p 9

There are a number of ways of practising wordless prayer, and Thomas Merton's advice at the head of this chapter reminds us that contemplative prayer is not about technique. It is a gift. We cannot control it; it is not an achievement of the ego. In fact it is one of the surest ways to defeat our obstinate egos. But there has to be some form of practice, regular and daily, so that we can quieten our everyday consciousness and move to the deepest level of our being. Centering Prayer is based on the words of Jesus recorded in Matthew, when he says:

> When you pray go into your inner room, and when you have shut the door, pray to your Father in secret, and the Father, who sees everything done in secret will reward you.[22]

Wordless prayer, or Centering Prayer, is a response to the invitation of the Holy Spirit. Although we have to make a conscious decision to pray in this way, it is only because of the invitation that often unexpectedly breaks out in our hearts and requires an answer. It urges us to deepen our friendship with the God within. Jesus invites us to move to that level of intimacy where God is experienced not as a distant judge, but a loving, caring and very tender presence. He will also be experienced at times as absent, but that is all part of the purifying process of love in which we are led from seeking the consolations of God into seeking the God of consolations. Contemplative prayer moves us beyond the seeking of signs, wonders and miracles in our spiritual life. Throughout the gospel Jesus keeps trying to move people's faith and trust beyond the evidence of wonderful signs to a deeper and purer level.

Mindful of Merton's warning of not getting caught up in technique let us take a closer look at some guidelines for the practice of contemplative prayer, basing them on the teaching of Jesus in chapter six of Matthew's gospel. Many teachers suggest twenty minutes as a good period of time for a daily practice. Whatever our duties in life most people can usually manage that.

Go into your private room

This first step requires that we withdraw from the ordinary flow of psychological awareness and move to a deeper level. The inner room is a symbol of the core of our being where we can escape from the fascinating display which constantly stimulates our senses throughout the course of a day. We let go of the noise and the distraction of everything going on around us, as well as the thoughts in our heads, our memories and emotions, and our plans for the future. We move

---

[22] Mt 6:6

to a level of silence and quiet. We find a different state of consciousness as we become present to the spiritual level of our being. Our ordinary psychological state of consciousness includes all that we can see and hear and touch, as well as thoughts and emotions. Everyday we watch a kind of outward show and it is so powerful, we forget there is any other kind of awareness. That is why Jesus advises us to move to another room, our private, inner room, a place of peace and quiet. And just think how much external stimulation we have today in comparison with the time of Jesus.

Stillness

The next recommended guideline is to sit still. The back should be kept straight, eyes either closed or lowered to the ground, or perhaps focussed on a particular object. The feet should be on the ground and hands either gently touching, or open in a receptive gesture. If we experience distracting thoughts or images, then gently let them go. Our guiding attitude should be one of being open and receptive to all things. If there is noise in the room or outside, notice it for what it is, then gently return to a more focussed awareness. In Centering Prayer it is recommended to use a *sacred word* such as Jesus, or Spirit, or love or peace or something similar. Just use it once to return to a deeper life of awareness. Some teachers recommend becoming aware of breathing, in and out, and realising that each breath is a wonderful gift of God. This is my own preferred practice. Usually we are not conscious of our breathing, but it is a reminder that if God did not love us and sustain us in each moment with unconditional love, we would just cease to exist. There are many people totally unaware of this love; in wordless prayer we want to connect with this deepest reality of our being, which participates in the very being of God. As the practice develops then you find yourself more aware during the day of breathing in God's life and love. It has a very calming effect and tunes into that deeper level of consciousness of the gift of Being that we all share.

This practice of stillness really grounds us in an ever-deepening experience of oneness with God and with everything that exists. It is perfectly possible to spend the whole period of wordless prayer in attending to your body and it would be a wonderful prayer. As Jesus says, we don't have to use many words like the pagans; all we have to do is to become present, conscious and aware of the gift of Being. We don't really have to do anything; it is just a case of loving attention to God in our hearts. For this to happen we do need silence and stillness as we switch off the noise and restless activity of our ordinary psychological awareness.

For too long, in our Christian spirituality, we have neglected the body as we struggle to overcome the damage done by distorted teachings that have tried to promote the spirit by downgrading the body. This is dualism at its worst. As we learn to sit in stillness we discover that our bodies are the gateway to God. This is truly incarnational spirituality as we honour the wonderful gesture of Jesus in taking on a human body.

This sitting in stillness can also have clear health benefits for the body. It helps to lower blood pressure and create a sense of peace and tranquillity. There is a lessening of Beta waves, the thinking part of the brain where the ego holds sway. Our need for boundaries and defences against others gives way to a deeper sense of unity and communion. This is gradual emergence of *the true self*. We start to re-discover our original self which is united at the level of Being with all creation. We are learning to see reality as it truly is without the preconceived judgements of the calculating defensive mind. Stillness and silence is a precious gift which our western society seems to fear. Recently in the United States I visited some wonderful bookstores, but all of them have relentless background music, not to mention the ubiquitous and intrusive mobile phone. Private conversations are transmitted loudly to all and sundry. There is no privacy now. Here in the UK it is being proposed to end the tradition of silence in public libraries. We seem to be threatened by silence.

Close the Door

There were no mobile phones in the time of Jesus, but he stressed the need to create privacy and quiet when he advises us to close the door of our inner room when praying. Some translations say *lock the door* which is perhaps Jesus' way of reminding us that the ego does not like to sit in silence *doing nothing*. It will suggest all kinds of much more important things we could be doing; calls to make, people to see, letters to write, whatever. Jesus suggests that we really need to shut ourselves off from the clamour of our everyday thoughts and emotions so that we can enter a deeper space. The question will arise, *what happens when thoughts and emotions clamour for our attention during wordless prayer?* The first thing to realise is that they certainly will. We cannot completely close down our monkey minds, which love to swing from thought to thought, or emotion to emotion. Prayer is not about not having distractions; it is about what we do with them.

If we can remain open and receptive in our prayer we need not be too perturbed by distractions. Try not to fight them because they will feed off oppositional energy and just grow stronger. Thomas Keating has a useful exercise to help here. Imagine you are sitting by a river, which represents your unconscious. Each distraction is like a boat floating down the river. You might get distracted by an argument you have just had with someone, or be thinking of an appointment you have later in the day. Once you become aware of the distraction, name it and identify it, but then very gently let it go. There is all the difference in the world between having an emotion and becoming possessed by an emotion. Awareness, consciousness, is the key to letting go and then returning your loving attention to God. Once you become aware that you are distancing yourself from the thought or the emotion, and lessening its control over you, then you can revert to your sacred word, or simply your breathing, to refocus your attention. The sacred word or your breathing is your way of consenting to the contemplative process.

Do not get upset by distractions. It is impossible to avoid them and the ego will always fight your attempts to sit in stillness. In fact, the ego cannot live in the present moment, which is the heart of all contemplative practice. Ego consciousness will either take you back to past events or forward to the future. It cannot deal with the now, because there is nothing to fix or achieve. Wordless prayer invites us to experience the present moment, the now, or *the eternal now* as it has always been called in religious language.

Most people are totally captivated by the mind. It is a truly wonderful instrument, but it is not the whole picture. It is an instrument to be used in the right way as a servant of consciousness not the master. In his recent bestseller, Eckhart Tolle critiques the philosophy of Descartes for being so damaging in this respect. Descartes equated *thinking* with *being*. Eckhart addresses the knower or the watcher behind the thinker. This knowing awareness is a liberating step that moves us from being controlled by our mind to becoming more truly present and conscious:

> When you listen to a thought, you are aware not only of the thought but also of yourself as the witness of the thought. A new dimension of consciousness has come in. As you listen to the thought, you feel a conscious presence – your deeper self – behind or underneath the thought as it were. The thought then loses its power over you and quickly subsides, because you are no longer energising the mind through identification with it. This is the beginning and the end of involuntary and compulsive thinking.[23]

[23] Eckhart Tolle *The Power Of Now* (Hodder & Stoughton London 2005) p 15

Tolle is a not a Christian theologian, but what he is teaching is the *process* of how to live in the now which goes right back to the Greek and Latin tradition of wordless contemplation, and has usually been called the *apophatic* way. This way of praying without words or concepts, or emotions is in contrast to the *cataphatic* tradition, which relies on words, images and symbols in what most people understand and practice as discursive meditation. This apophatic tradition is being recovered today. It doesn't have to replace the cataphatic tradition, the two should be used together; but it is the purer form of prayer and seems best suited to deal with the oppositional, calculating and dualistic mind, which sees everything in terms of either/or, black or white, good or bad.

In Secret

For Christians the point of entering our inner room is to experience the Father of Jesus as an intimate loving presence made available to us by the action of the Holy Spirit. We experience total acceptance by a Merciful and Compassionate God upon whom we depend for every aspect of our being. Thomas Keating describes this merciful action as *Divine Therapy* offered to us in the secrecy of our hearts. In therapy we project our pain and woundedness onto a compassionate therapist who assures us that we are basically lovable. Nothing can give greater consolation than to be fully accepted by a God who is not there to punish or judge us but who loves us unconditionally. I remember preaching about this in a Retreat to priests in California. A former Provincial said that he liked what I was saying but asked how to respond to those who remind us about God's justice, as well as his mercy. Fortunately I had with me my copy of Pope Benedict's encyclical, *God is Love*, so I referred him to these words:

> God's passionate love for his people – for humanity – is at the same time a forgiving love. It is so great that it turns God against himself, his love against his justice.[24]

The Pope is speaking the language of the mystics who speak constantly about God's compassionate love and mercy. God's love is so powerful that it overwhelms his justice and turns it into mercy and forgiveness.

As we experience this mercy and love at the core of our being during wordless prayer, we also experience something more painful and testing. Human beings are a mixed blessing: we are at the same time both original blessing and original sin. The blessing is foundational but we can never escape the wounds of our

---

[24] Pope Benedict XVI *God is Love* (CTS London 2006) p 14

human condition. They may have been caused by our parents, or by others, but any experience of pain and rejection goes deep and is stored in the unconscious and in our bodies. In contemplative prayer those kinds of hurts will come to the surface. They are the scars and wounds that keep us locked into our defensive posture before others, and I will say more of this later. Suffice it to say, at this point, that God will heal some of these wounds gradually over time. We might prefer to have all our hurts healed, but, as we discover, our woundedness becomes a surprise entry-point into much deeper spiritual growth. In fact, they are a necessary part of the spiritual journey. But this is not easy to accept at first and may explain why many do not want to embark on the contemplative journey. We prefer our religion as a belonging system, a badge of honour, a set of beliefs and rituals that prevent us having to change in any radical and fundamental way. The ego is very content with such a view of religion, but in fact it is based on a lie.

The key to mature spirituality is unmasking this lie; a lie based on a false sense of religious identity. We don't know who we really are.

Chapter Four
The Great Discovery

The chief thing that separates us from God is the
thought that we are separated from Him. If we
get rid of that thought, our troubles will be greatly
reduced. We fail to believe that we are always with
God and that he is part of every reality. The present
moment, every object we see, our inmost nature, all
are rooted in Him. But we hesitate to believe this
until personal experience gives us the confidence to
believe in it.[25]

---

[25] Thomas Keating *Open Mind Open Heart* (The Continuum Publishing Company NY 1997) p 44

Searchers for God have always been attracted by pilgrimages. They seem to provide easier access to the spiritual dimension of life. The physical journey acts out and images the deeper spiritual journey. The enduring popularity of shrines such as Lourdes and Fatima confirms the experiences of many who feel closer to God and the numinous at such places. I remember a pilgrim returning from Iona in Scotland. Asked about the experience, she said, *The air is thinner there*. I'm sure these experiences are genuine and, in the rather frenetic atmosphere in which we live, they provide the opportunity to access the deeper levels of the spirit, which our extraverted and noisy world too often excludes.

The recovery of the contemplative tradition is bringing the search for God home. The great insight is that God dwells within. We don't have to travel great distances to find God; we are found by God. This is the vision of the poet T S Eliot who speaks of our journeys ending where we began. What has changed is that we have learned to see in a new way. The poets and the mystics have always known this and it is well expressed by the eighteenth century English poet William Blake who was poet, mystic and artist rolled into one:

> If the doors of perception are cleansed everything would appear to
> man as it is, infinite. For man has closed himself up till he sees all
> things thro' narrow chinks of his cavern.[26]

Blake is suggesting that the means of seeing are already present within us. All we have to do is cleanse the doors of perception to see everything touched by infinity. Blake's words go to the heart of the religious search which doesn't require any physical journey at all, however helpful that might be. The doors of perception are best cleansed by contemplative prayer.

There is quite a lot of tension today between formal religion in its institutional form and spirituality. Many moderns and postmoderns like to identify themselves as spiritual, but not religious. They sense a spiritual dimension to life but don't want to identify with Church practice, creeds and rituals. I discussed this issue in my last book[27] and I think that it points to weaknesses on both sides of the argument. If the spiritual is pursued as a private quest for inner bliss it loses the essentially communal aspect of the journey to God. A relational God in a relational world such as the quantum physicists are revealing, cannot be reached by an isolated spiritual enterprise. It is too cosy a world and it refuses to face the fundamental fact that we are social beings. Crucially it keeps the ego firmly in place and, often, keeps the poor at arm's length. An ego-controlled spiritual

---

[26] William Blake *Selected* Poetry ed. Michael Mason (Oxford University Press 2008) p 80
[27] Michael Cunningham *Lost & Found* (Don Bosco Publications UK 2007)

search will not lead to any real transformation. It bolsters the small self and keeps the world of pain and suffering, of poverty and injustice at a distance. A private spiritual search will never heal our fragmented world; it simply reinforces the divisions between rich and poor. There is no change of consciousness. When Jesus begins his teaching and healing ministry, he called a group of disciples to work and live with him, to emphasise that this journey is communal as well as personal. It is essentially relational. For William Blake the *doors of perception* open out onto a deeply connected and inter-dependent world, not a private heaven in a private cavern.

On the other hand, institutional religion often blocks the process of transformation by emphasising behaviour rather than perception: what I do is much more important than how I see. My doing is much more important than my Being. The central error here, as Thomas Keating's quotation at the head of the chapter makes clear, is to see God as separate and apart, usually described as *up there*, in heaven. Religion then becomes the means to get me from *here* where I am, to *there* where God is supposed to dwell. So I have to discover the right rituals, the right behaviour and the right doctrines that will get me to God, or to save my individual soul, as it is usually expressed. Religion includes the social dimension of faith as it gathers communities of worship, but the danger is to see my particular group as the in-group, the chosen group who are on the way to heaven, while other groups, including other religions, will find it much more difficult. This is religion as a belonging system; religion for the first half of life. It is an important and necessary stage, but it is only the beginning of the journey. Here also the ego stays in control and even prayer becomes a way of manipulating God.

Ken Wilber suggests that religion should perform two necessary but very different functions in the spiritual journey. The first stage is to provide meaning for the separate self, and it does this through rituals to perform, doctrines to believe, and moral directives to guide behaviour. This is the essential first stage of the journey; the problem is that, too often, it becomes the whole journey. It is very attractive because it allows us to think of ourselves as being very dedicated, very good, very moral and very pious. We all want that! The problem is that this kind of religion doesn't really offer any real transformation or change of consciousness. It keeps the religious *false self* firmly in place. A number of surveys have demonstrated that religious believers are no more altruistic than non-believers. That should make us think. What this religion seems to be doing is reinforcing the small self. It defends and protects the ego, even though it might be a religious ego. Religious egos are very difficult to eradicate, as Jesus discovered in his many battles with righteous, law-abiding people.

Wilber maintains that this kind of religion is the majority position. He suggests, however, that the real purpose of religion is not to reinforce and strengthen the separate self, but to break it apart and shatter it. In this he underlines why the great spiritual teachers describe the spiritual journey as a descent not an ascent. They speak of emptiness, poverty, letting go, surrender, the way of the cross. There is a very significant moment when Jesus seems to be becoming very popular and the crowds following him are getting very large:

> When the crowds were increasing, he began to say, *This generation is an evil generation; it asks for a sign, but no sign will be given to it except the sign of Jonah.*[28]

These are very challenging words from Jesus; he even describes the crowd's desire for signs as evil. Many religious believers still look for signs in our confusing world today. Jesus offers only one sign: the journey of Jonah who spent three days in the belly of the whale and then was spat out to a new life, a new kind of consciousness. Here we have Jesus speaking about the one and only sign he will give. This is his own metaphor for his own journey through suffering and death, leading to the new life of the Resurrection. Far from bolstering the ordinary consciousness of the small self that wants to feel good about itself, Jesus is pointing to a radical transformation into a new consciousness at the level of soul, a new creation, a new way of being.

This dying process may seem, to many, as off-putting, but it is dying into a richer experience of life. It is the difference between watching a film in black and white and watching in colour. The whole purpose is to transform the small self into a much larger and more truthful identity. It leads to a different sense of *I*, one that lives in a more spacious, expansive place filled with love and compassion for all. This is the great discovery of who I really am, this is *the pearl of great price, the treasure hidden in the field*, the goal of the spiritual search. This is the moment of transformation that reveals what spiritual teachers call *the true self*. It is the fullness of life and marked by a decisive shift from self-centeredness to God-centeredness. We discover that, contrary to our *common sense* view, we are not separate from God, but living in God. We are clearly not God, but our life is sustained at every moment by God, as our loving Creator. This is what it means to be made in the image and likeness of God. This is what Jesus revealed throughout his ministry when he said that his Father and He would come to live in us.

---

[28] Mt 12:39

When spiritual teachers describe *the false self* as an illusion they are describing the parts of me that prevent this process happening. The autonomous self distorts my true identity: God created me to become a fully-aware person. Whatever prevents me from being my true self is therefore false: selfishness, pride, fear, judgementalism, my desire to build walls that protect me from others, especially those I don't like or those I don't agree with. This is the root of the fragmented view that holds such sway in our world. At a deeper level it also includes the parts of myself that I don't like, what is normally called the shadow. The lines of division lie both within and without. This is the stranglehold of fear, which is the opposite of love.

This is a decisive step in the spiritual life. Too much religion suggests that we have to exclude, reject, expel or deny the contaminating element. Real spiritual growth happens when we can embrace, accept and forgive the wounded part of our being. God has given us the very means to do this: prayer and suffering. Prayer is not one more duty to be completed on our journey to God. To pray is to participate in the very life of God. We don't have to initiate prayer. We are simply joining in the flow of mutual love that flows continually between Father, Son and Spirit. St Paul points this out in Chapter Eight of his letter to the Romans. He begins by describing the new reality of who we are in God:

> There is therefore now no condemnation for those who are in Christ Jesus. For the law of the Spirit of life in Christ Jesus has set you free from the law of sin and death.[29]

For Paul this is the new creation, the new consciousness, the transforming gift of union. As for Jesus, it is all about union. Paul goes on to speak about how this union operates in prayer:

> The Spirit helps us in our weakness; for we do not know how to pray as we ought, but that very spirit intercedes with sighs too deep for words. And God, who searches the heart, knows what is in the mind of the Spirit.[30]

This is what Jesus alludes to when he tells us to enter our inner room and open ourselves to the self-giving love and mutuality in the life of the Trinity which happens *in secret*. in the depths of our being.

In this union with God, our true self emerges, the particular personality that God

---

[29] Rom 8:1
[30] Rom 8:26-27

has given us. Union doesn't mean uniformity. We are all unique and different, and yet deeply united in the Being of God. This Being of God is essentially relational. It is described by the word *Trinity*, and thankfully, today theologians are recovering the foundational relatedness of this mystery. Just as the quantum physicists are revealing the essential relatedness of sub-atomic world, so our theologians are bringing us home to the central mystery of God as Inter-Being: Three Persons in one union of love and mutual self-giving and receiving. This cleansing of the doors of our perception allows us to see the gift of Being for what it is: the *really real*. Once we die to our limited view of ourselves as separate private individuals we recognise the image of God in all things and in all people.

In this new consciousness, God is no longer perceived as *out there* in splendid isolation. The incarnation of Jesus means that everything is touched by the grace and the glory of God. God's transcendence has flowed into his immanence. We can no longer think of God as a separate *Object* among other lesser objects. God is the *Ground of everything* that exists. God is the source and foundation of everything. God is in everything and everything reflects God. Contemplation means coming to full awareness and consciousness of this vision of reality. Awareness is directly related to a sense of my true identity in God. Once I recognise and accept this, the next – and crucial – step is to accept this image in others, and especially in places and people where I find it difficult and challenging.

This is why contemplative practice is so important because it reveals our true identity. All of us are born with the potential to be contemplatives. Many never awaken to this core aspect of their reality and live with no conscious awareness of who they really are. The treasure remains hidden in the field, but once we discover this treasure within us, as Jesus said, everything else is placed in proper perspective. Under the influence of the Holy Spirit we become more aware of the contemplative dimension of our true selves. This gift reveals the great mystery of Being that surrounds us at all times. we can then move beyond dualistic categories of sacred and secular. As Merton teaches, *Everything that exists is holy*.

This new consciousness sees the unity in all things. It is a different sense of self. The transformation is perfectly described by Paul when he says, *I live no longer, Christ lives in me*. This may not be apparent or obvious because Paul says our lives are *hidden* with Christ in God. This transformation meets the divisions and boundaries which we set up between ourselves and others, whether it is someone we are living with in family or community, or another group of people, race or religion that we disapprove of. The notion of religion as a belonging system that puts me and my group in a superior position has to die. This is not easy, and it does involve real suffering as our sense of gravity shifts to the new consciousness. How does this transformation happen? It is not something we can achieve; it is the work of Christ. This is what we mean by *salvation*. It is revealed in the mystery of cross and Resurrection. This is what Christ does for us.

Our divided fragmented world mirrors our divided fragmented selves. What we fear in ourselves we project onto others. This projection often takes the form of violence. It may be physical violence so evident in wars and torture of other human beings, or it may be emotional violence in the way we control, dominate others or judge them as inferior. Rene Girard has revealed the centrality of the scapegoat mechanism at the heart of human history. If we can find someone to blame it seems to assuage our need for violence. Every religion in human history has done this at some time or other. Jesus identifies with all human victims, he becomes the ultimate victim of history. Condemned by Herod and Pilate, Jesus is rejected by both religion and politics. But it is what happens with his followers, which most reveals the saving, forgiving love of God.

The Jewish people had learned over a long period to reject other protective gods and to rely on one God, Yahweh. They expected and prayed that he would save them from all harm. He would be their God, more powerful and more almighty than any other tribal god. To their amazement and disappointment they fell into very difficult situations: slavery in Egypt; a long journey of forty years through the Sinai wilderness; exile into Babylon; and in the time of Jesus, occupation by the Romans. Then Jesus appears; preaching about God not with images of power and domination, but as a loving and forgiving father. But his followers clearly expected him to drive out the Romans and restore the kingdom of Israel and they would get the positions of power and influence. Even the mother of James and John thought the same way. The disciples clearly had their scapegoats and they asked Jesus to call down fire and brimstone on the despised Samaritans. Jesus reacts by making the Samaritan the hero of one of his most famous stories; but they still could not see. When he predicted his suffering and death they rejected what he said and fled when it all happened, with Peter denying any knowledge of Jesus.

What Jesus does on the cross is to accept totally the betrayal of his friends and the violence of his enemies and transform them into forgiveness and compassion. We need to see our own complicity in this event. Our fear and rejection of ourselves and others is what we crucify in Jesus. The other, the stranger, the people I don't like, the parts of my own life that I repress are all absorbed by this extraordinary act of forgiveness.

> Father, forgive them; for they do not know what they are doing.[31]

We cannot transform *our false self*, that would be another self-referenced ego achievement. It is Christ who achieves this for us as Paul reminds us:

> He died for all, so that those who live might live no longer for themselves, but for him who died and was raised for them.[32]

When the risen Jesus meets the friends who abandoned and betrayed him he makes no reference to this at all. When they are locked in fear in the upper room, he breathes the gift of forgiveness on them. When he meets them on the shore of the lake he makes breakfast for them. He reminds Peter, the man who denied him, that it is all about love. On the road to Emmaus, the hearts of the disciples are burning as they encounter the loving fire of the Risen Jesus. For these disciples everything changes, as it does for us, when we see the depths of God's forgiveness of our self-centred lives, and the invitation to live as new creations, centred in God, not the half-life of the separate individualistic self.

This is a new way of seeing, a new way of being; it is living out of a new consciousness. All we have to do is to say *Yes* which is the act of faith and it changes the way we view not just ourselves but everyone else.

> From now on, therefore, we regard no one from a human point of view, even though we once knew Christ from a human point of view, we know him no longer in that way. So if anyone is in Christ there is a new creation: everything old has passed away; see everything has become new! All this is from God, who reconciled us to himself through Christ, and has given us the ministry of reconciliation; that is, in Christ, God was reconciling the world to himself, not counting their trespasses against them, and entrusting the message of reconciliation to us.[33]

When Paul says that he no longer sees anyone from a human point of view he means a *merely* human point of view, because we are offered this new life in Christ through faith. This doesn't take away our humanity; it transforms it.

---

[31] Lk 23:34
[32] 2 Cor 5:15
[33] 2 Cor 5:16-18

The paschal mystery of Christ is continually at work in our flawed yet glorious humanity. *Our false self* never goes away completely; Christ is present in us in the form of crucified love. *The true self* shares the glory of the Risen Christ, who makes it possible for us to become agents of reconciliation in our fragmented world that is crying out for healing and for newness. Contemplative prayer and some experience of suffering create a new spaciousness in our hearts where compassion replaces judgement. This new way of being goes beyond either/or, right and wrong, us and them, into a unified vision for a broken humanity that is at the same time touched by the infinite.

Chapter Five
Different Ways of Seeing

A system based in duality can't possibly perceive oneness;
it can't create anything beyond itself
– only more duality and more trouble.
So the drama goes on and on.
But we do have the capacity, if we so choose,
to shift to a whole different basis of perception.[34]

---

[34] Cynthia Bourgeault *The Wisdom Jesus* (Shambhala Publications Ltd USA 2008) p 35

This insight of Cynthia Bourgeault opens up an issue which is receiving more attention with the work of Claire Graves, Don Beck and Ken Wilbur in the area of consciousness. It seems that there are different levels of consciousness. What James Fowler discovered in the area of faith, and Lawrence Kohlberg and Carol Gilligan in the matter of morality, is that not everyone is at the same level. You could hardly equate Hitler's level of moral awareness with Mother Theresa's. Although the study of consciousness is relatively new, Jesus was clearly aware of this problem. In his parable of the Sower, he points out how different people respond to the word at different levels. For some, the level may be very shallow; with others, it takes deeper roots. Faced by his passion and death even his closest followers abandoned him. The breakthrough to a deeper level of spiritual consciousness, to a true understanding of the paschal mystery needed the dramatic appearance of the Holy Spirit in the form of wind and fire upon the fearful apostles. It is the Spirit that transforms everything and is doing the same work in our souls today.

This is why contemplative prayer is so valuable for all those involved in active ministry. We have seen how first-stage religion tends to bolster and strengthen the ego, but the real purpose of religion is to shatter that experience of the separate self. The mystical insight is very simple, but mind shattering: it is the essential unity of all things. All is One and One is all. We live and move and have our being in the Ground of all Being that we call God. Once this is grasped everything changes. It is indeed a transformation of consciousness. The principal effect is to break down the barriers and boundaries that the ego builds up to protect the private self. This doesn't mean that we lose our individuality, but the ego ceases to be the great controlling influence; it is part of a greater whole, not the whole deal as we often think. Spiritual writers use the phrase *egocentric mind* to describe *our egocentric way of looking at things*. The egocentric mind is basically defensive; it sees and judges everything from the position of private advantage. What's in it for me? How will this affect me? What the Spirit does is to break down the defensive barriers of our egocentric mindset.

Spiritual teachers are telling us that we are at a vital stage in our world today when we need to move from self-centred living to other-centred living. There will be enormous resistance to this because we not only have to confront the private ego but also the collective ego, what we in our contemporary language call the system, the way things are. That is why our times are being called a second axial age, an age of profound change with enormous consequences for all of us on this planet. Plenty of evidence suggests that the Spirit of God is touching the hearts of many people today and the deeply traditional form of prayer we call contemplative prayer is being rediscovered in our time. Nothing else can free us from the limitations of the egocentric mindset.

The first axial age ran from 800 to 200 BCE and, not unlike our own, it was a time of profound change. It was the Iron Age when new and more destructive weaponry emerged, nothing like as destructive as our times, but still causing fear and apprehension. At the same time it marked the emergence of the individual from the tribal ethic. There was a turning to the *self*, and this greater degree of reflection led to the foundation of the great religions of the world: Confucianism in China, monotheism in Israel, Hinduism and Buddhism in India. At the same time Greek civilisation promoted the importance of reason. Today we face a similar significant challenge. Just as the first axial age moved from tribal to individual consciousness so we today are being challenged to move to a global consciousness and awareness. Our world has become dramatically changed at so many levels. For good or bad it has become smaller:

> Today we are making another quantum leap forward. Our technology has created a global society, which is interconnected electronically, militarily, economically, and politically. We now have to develop a global consciousness, because whether we like it or not, we live in one world.[35]

Karen Armstrong rightly argues that this is happening whether we like it or not. The first axial age produced extraordinary religious creativity and something similar is being asked of us today. A global spiritual consciousness can only happen if we can see beyond the defences and barriers that are no longer serving our world well.

Religious differences can be just as dangerous as political differences and rivalries. I recently saw an interview on television news with a young newly-married female would-be suicide bomber. She is Palestinian. When she was asked how she could justify killing Jewish women and children she had no hesitation: they might be innocent now, but they could become combatants. So trapped inside the logic of her fundamentalism the solution was simple: kill them now. As might be expected she ended the interview by explaining that she was doing it all for God. Her new husband was sitting beside her, clearly approving her action. There is so much mindless violence and ignorant killing taking place in our world both at the level of individuals such as this sadly deluded young woman, and at the level of nations and governments who propose war as a solution to problems.

---

[35] Karen Armstrong *The Great Transformation* (Atlantic Books London 2007) p 397

The egocentric mindset is quick to justify such violence whether in the name of *my people, my tribe, my religion, my country,* or, worst of all, *my God.*

A global consciousness will lead us beyond these dangerous divisions. We need to move beyond the dualism of the egocentric mind that sees everything as separate. A new, more evolutionary understanding of the person is at the heart of this change. We need to become what Paul called *new creations.* In our times the creative energy of the Holy Spirit is touching people at a deep level. The Christian Churches have tended to emphasise the externals of religion, the rules and regulations, the doctrines and the rituals. While not neglecting these, there is a growing hunger today for transformation from within. As we saw in the last chapter, religious belief and practice can sometimes reinforce *the false self.* Many religious believers want to remain in control and in charge of their lives. We find the idea of surrendering the private self as very threatening.

The paschal mystery of Christ invites us to make the journey of surrender, to give up clinging to our false needs for security and a good reputation. When people fall in love, the boundaries and defences that ring-fence our hearts, in what might be called ordinary consciousness, are broken down. It is an exhilarating experience and opens up new dimensions of life, joy and energy. It also, of course, opens the heart to the vulnerability of an intimate relationship. What we forget is that God is love, the source and energy behind all love. This is the kind of relationship God wants with human beings. All God wants from us is the surrender of our hearts: in that act lies the discovery of our true self which participates in the unity of Being, that is God. Where all creatures participate in this gift of Being unconsciously, we humans are at the high point of evolution and in the whole of creation we alone can participate consciously and willingly in the relational gift of Being.

The shift that is required is from seeing ourselves as separate, to a sense of communion at the level of Being. This new consciousness breaks down the barriers in how we perceive ourselves and other people. Rather than concentrating on the differences, we move to the unitive level of being.

Students of consciousness are suggesting that there are different levels of awareness, of consciousness. Richard Rohr,[36] in a talk given at York University in 2007, suggested that six levels have been identified and the progression is from lower more dualistic levels of thinking and perceiving to higher non-dualistic stages. The word dualism is rooted in the western philosophical tradition. This

---

[36] Richard Rohr *On the Edge* (CD published by Agape Ministries Southport UK 2008)

is the binary mindset which sees everything as either/or, black or white, right or wrong. It sees everything in competition and by comparison: this is not that; that is not this. This is the view that triumphed at the Reformation and the Enlightenment and almost killed off the contemplative tradition. It is the way most of us view the world. In contrast the mystical path moves beyond dualisms to embrace paradox. Authentic religion has always promoted the need for paradox because life is more mystery than a set of problems to be solved. So the Catholic Church affirms Jesus as fully God and fully human. We proclaim Mary to be both virgin and mother. Yet our everyday consciousness remains dualistic: inside and outside, right and wrong, either/or.

Paradox, on the other hand, reveals that two apparent opposites do not always cancel each other out. They can both be true at the same time; and a deeper truth emerges. Today the quantum world is saying exactly that. The classic example is Light, which appears as a wave and a particle; both are true at the same time. The binary mind cannot deal with this. So we seem to be suggesting that higher levels of consciousness allow us to deal with the complexities of life, as there is nothing so complex as the human person. The practice of contemplative awareness opens the mind up to this deeper level of non-dual awareness. The mystics of all the great religions agree on this, and the coming together of East and West in recent years is one of the great signs of the times.

Our consciousness moves through six identifiable levels that lead from information-gathering to transformation. What is vital to remember is that each stage builds on the next one which includes and deepens the level of awareness. We can't get to wisdom and transformation with information and knowledge.

1. Information

We all begin by acquiring information, with the gathering of facts and data. Everyone starts here, but many stay locked at this level. We need to be able to identify and name things, but what tends to happen is that facts feed our ego and before long we begin to argue: my facts are better than your facts. This competitive, oppositional thinking goes deep especially in our western culture. Clever people love to operate here. The problem is that you can be very good at gathering information and facts, without acquiring an ounce of wisdom. We have an enormous amount of information available in our culture, but as we saw with the war in Iraq, information without wisdom can have such tragic consequences. But this kind of technique and mastery of facts often gets richly rewarded. The problem is that it is a power game. Love of power and influence surpasses the search for truth and wisdom.

2. Knowledge

The key to this next level is the discernment of patterns. These are the engineers, the scientists, the experts in various fields. They solve problems and are extremely useful in our technological society. If your car breaks down, you have to find someone who is able to fix it. Likewise with so many of the machines that make our lives so much easier. While this kind of knowledge is so useful and practical it tended to affect the way we approached religion, which ought to lead us into the world of mystery.

But the desire to control mystery rather than surrender to it, often reduced the role of many clergy to what Richard Rohr calls *the mechanisation of mystery*. Priests became experts at measuring, organising and managing religion. Differences between mortal and venial sins were carefully measured; liturgy was reduced to strict observance of the ritual; prayer, as we have seen, was reduced to *saying prayers*. We had the whole industry of indulgences, novenas, and the great insurance policy of the nine First Fridays. In this kind of religious outlook there was no mention of the need for transformation. The emphasis was on the external performances of religion.

The Catholic Church has been particularly strong in this style of religion, because of our hierarchical structure. The teaching of contemplative prayer virtually disappeared. The sense of mystery went with it: the priest was the man who had an answer for everything. We forgot that what Jesus taught was a process – the paschal mystery – not a set of conclusions. We Catholics always claimed to have the correct answers. Our facts were better than other religions' facts. Without any inner experience of what was truly real through contemplative prayer, the externalisation of religion was complete. We filled people's heads rather than fed their souls. The care of souls was often reduced to quantification and measurement. It was an exercise in control.

3. Intelligence

Traditionally great theologians like Thomas Aquinas and Duns Scotus made an important distinction between two types of intelligence: analytic/rational intelligence, and intuitive/co-natural intelligence. What does this mean?

a. Analytic/Rational

Good intelligence will lead to seeing bigger patterns, learning to think outside the box, and the ability to make connections. Rational, analytic intelligence has largely held sway in the Church since the enlightenment, mainly because the

Church found itself fighting opponents. Once you set out to defeat an opponent you tend to become like them. This only bolsters the egocentric mind and leads to a desire to win the argument rather than discover the truth. Again, without inner experience, this is almost inevitable. The stress is on externals: rules and regulations, forms and rituals, shaped by dualistic consciousness. There is little room for transformation. Analytic intelligence lives in the head.

What these first three and a half stages have in common is that they are primarily involved in *measuring* reality. The shift to a higher consciousness occurs with the move to *meeting* reality. When I am measuring, my ego is still in control. When I truly engage and meet another person, or *the Other*, my ego has to get out of the way. This is why contemplation is described as a different way of perceiving and looking at reality.

b. Intuitive/Co-natural

This is the crossover point that marks the real shift from religion to spirituality. It is the move from measuring reality to meeting. As Martin Buber once said, *All real living is attending.* This is where contemplation begins to bear fruit as a different way of seeing. It sees reality as it is, and doesn't try to shape or manipulate it to meet my limited perspective, my egocentric mind. Contemplation is the poetry of religion. It cleanses the doors of perception as Blake suggests. It allows us to see the infinite in the ordinary.

The word *co-natural* is important here in describing this kind of intelligence. All of us have a built in programme for recognising the Divine. It is the mystics who are most attuned to this level of awareness. Just consider some of these statements: Julian of Norwich, *Our souls are knitted into God.* Catherine of Genoa: *My deepest me is God.* St Augustine: *You have made us for yourselves Lord, and our heart is restless until it rests in you.* Meister Eckhart: *God shines in all things.* In our modern parlance we would say that our deepest DNA is God, or as we say colloquially, *it takes one to know one.* That is what is meant by the statement at the beginning of Genesis that all of humanity is made in the image and likeness of God. When Jesus met people he would ask them, *Who do you say I am?* What this question really means is *What is it in you that recognises me, what is it that connects you with me?* We are talking here about *recognition*; once it has happened, it opens up a whole new way of seeing. This kind of recognition, as we shall see later, is rooted in the heart, or more accurately *the eye of the heart*, that is the presence of the Spirit in us.

4. Understanding

This higher level of awareness teaches us that we cannot control the mystery; we can only stand in wonder. This is not easy for many of us especially in our culture which idolises control. We hear so many people saying, *I've got to take control of my life*. Psychologically this may contain helpful truth, but at this level of the spiritual journey it will block any further growth. This is why we speak of a real dying to self, for *the true self* to emerge. The further you travel along this path, the less you may understand. Not many people are prepared for this since it calls for genuine surrender. This kind of knowing is a real unknowing, which is the challenging path the classic spiritual writer of *The Cloud of Unknowing* invites us to walk. It is, he suggests, a journey of bright darkness, an experience of poverty that gives us everything. Rational intelligence cannot take us on this journey; only love will do:

> Because he can certainly be loved, but not thought. He can be taken and held by love, but not by thought.[37]

The journey at this level moves into paradox. At times we may be led by the light of the Spirit; at other times by way of darkness. Both lead us to God. The Church has always recognised the limits of our rational, analytic intelligence in the distinction made between the gift of knowledge and the gift of wisdom in the gifts of the Holy Spirit.

5. Wisdom

At this stage the mind becomes the servant not the master. I think we have too often presented Jesus in terms of a moral teacher. Life is then understood as a struggle to climb the moral ladder. If we fail, God, who sees everything, will take note and then punish us. It is not a very joyous way of living, and it is certainly not good news. In my experience of Retreat Ministry all over the world I frequently speak to many whose image of God is still locked at this level. I honestly believe it is impossible to fall in love with this kind of dominant image. But Jesus is not a moralist; he is a wisdom teacher. We have tended to see religious teachers as either priests or prophets. We have neglected the third category, which was alive in the Near East culture at the time of Jesus, the wisdom teacher.

Just consider how Jesus actually taught his message, and I'm sure you will say: *by parables*. A parable is not a moral tale, as we have often presented it, but a style more akin to the Buddhist *koan*, which is a method of teaching that completely

---

[37] *The Cloud of Unknowing* (Paulist Press Mahwah NJ1981) Ch 6 p 130

changes our normal way of looking at things and perceiving things. In other words what Jesus is drawing us into is a radical change of consciousness. The shift is from the egocentric mind to seeing with the eye of the heart, with compassion, with mercy, with forgiveness.

6. Transformation

All the synoptic gospels agree that Jesus used the expression *the kingdom of God* to sum up his teaching. In John's gospel the phrase used is *eternal life*. At no stage does Jesus try to define what he means. He hints and suggests, *it is like this or it is like that* as he uses parables to move his listeners to ever deeper levels of awareness. He is clearly aware that not everyone is at the same level of understanding. The disciples themselves struggled with this new kind of wisdom and asked Jesus directly why he taught this way:

> *Why do you speak to them in parables?* He answered, *To you it has been given to know the secrets of the kingdom of heaven but to them it has not been given.*[38]

Later he explains why many of the crowd do not understand his teaching:

> *For these people's heart has grown dull.*[39]

Jesus suggests that authentic awareness is located not in the egocentric mind, but in the *heart*. We can only know the mysteries of the kingdom when we do our inner work.

This is why contemplative prayer is so important. We cannot achieve spiritual transformation by our own efforts. It is not an achievement; it is a gift. But what we can do is to create the condition for transformation to happen. That is why every spiritual teacher emphasises the importance of regular daily practice of prayer; because this kind of prayer moves us out of the compulsive patterns of the egocentric mind that reinforces our self-centred way of life. Without regular practice it is all too easy to slip back into the default mode of the egocentric mind. As we shall see, in the next chapter, the eye of the heart is a radical change that transforms everything. As transformation takes hold we learn to receive reality without judgement, without critique, but with the eyes of compassion and mercy.

[38] Mt 13:10-11
[39] v 15

Chapter Six
The Eye of the Heart

The heart of the Christian experience is a new
seeing: a seeing of ourselves, others, and the world,
in and through the love of God. All of this can be
understood and said in many ways but the central
theme is the same. The pulsating heartbeat is that
my life is no longer woven around a wounded
autonomous self but finds itself bathed and
anointed in the healing love of God.[40]

---

[40] Charles R Ringma *Hear the Heart Beat* (SPCK London 2006) p 45

The transformation of consciousness allows us to see everything differently. Our whole world-view and perspective changes from the separate existence of *the false self* to the larger, richer, more spacious life of *the true self*. In all spiritual traditions contemplative prayer seems to be the best way to experience this new mindset, always remembering that it is a gift of God, not the achievement of the ego. This invitation is offered by Jesus at the beginning of his ministry when he urges us to see the world through different eyes. He calls it *metanoia*, a radical change in the way we view reality. When Nicodemus, the thoughtful but tentative Pharisee, meets Jesus, under cover of darkness, he is told he has to undergo a whole new birth in water and in the Spirit if he is to enter the kingdom of God, which is Jesus' metaphor for what is *really real*. For Jesus it is not business as usual and Nicodemus doesn't seem to be able to grasp this new level of consciousness.

All Christians receive the gift of the Spirit at Baptism. The sacrament is a ritual acting-out of the death to *the false self* and an incorporation into the paschal journey of Jesus. We rise to the new life in Christ. We now participate in a new level of Being, but it has to be grasped at the level of consciousness, and this takes time. We all begin life as a bundle of physical and emotional needs, for food, for safety, and for love. We experience ourselves at the centre of these needs, and we see parents and others as meeting *what I want and what I need*. Hopefully these are met and, in particular, we can experience unconditional love, the most beautiful love in the world.

I mentioned in Chapter Two that, as we grow, our experience of love changes and our parents begin to place conditions on their love for us. They want to educate us properly and face social pressures to appear to be successful, so they begin to introduce conditions. *If you behave properly, if you do this or do that, then Mum and Dad will love you.* This is necessary but it can do real damage to the child's sense of worth. The child starts to think, *I am loved because of what I do, or when I behave, not really because of who I am.* We may even get punished physically when we do not meet these expectations. And so *the false self* crystallises around the need to defend myself against the world of other people, who are often viewed as threats to my welfare. What comes out of all this painful growth is that love is not really unconditional; it has to be earned.

Since our parents are our first educators in every way, this attitude transfers into the way we think of God. In the years of Retreat Ministry I have been involved in, I have met many people who still feel afraid of God. This is deep-rooted and explains, I think, why so many Christians may believe in God, may attend weekly worship, but they are not in love with God. They might even think it odd if you suggest they ought to be in love with God. This includes many priests and religious; they may be very happy to work for God, but they are not in love with God. They feel that's for saints, but not really for them. I know this is true because I have been through this experience myself. When I was first sent to Bootle, Merseyside, as a young priest I expected to be successful. As I mentioned in Chapter Three, I was neglecting my prayer life. The young people in that comprehensive school were challenging in many ways, but I was a Salesian, and I had dedicated my life to working for the young. I shared many of their interests: I liked football and music, and I had a good sense of humour. But it turned out to be much more difficult than I expected. I remember a boy saying to me one day in class, *You don't like us, Father.* I was really taken aback by this and asked him what he meant. He said, *In this class you are always looking at your watch.* He was right. I was counting down the minutes till I could get away from that difficult group of children and teach more biddable ones. That taught me a lesson. It also made me question my motives. Was I working for the love of God, or for my own pride and glory? It was a blow for my ego and one that I needed to experience. Yes, I think I was working for God, but I wasn't prepared to spend any time with God in prayer. I thought I had more important things to do.

The problem is that we think that we have to earn God's love by the way we behave and live. In fact none of us can ever be worthy of God's love. It is not about worthiness; it is pure gift. It has to be received not achieved. In normal everyday circumstances we try to hide our worst side from others. We want to look good, even if we know that we are not that good. *Our false self* can get quite good at this, as we build a strong, independent, autonomous self, protected by the ego. The way we look at others, and the world in general, is then forced into this defensive world-view. I have my circle of friends, but beyond that, so many others are perceived as a threat to me. We identify ourselves with what we have, what we can do, and what others think of us. It is our face to the world. When we introduce ourselves to others we invariably tell them what we do, and what is our role or position. We build this false identity on external things. At times we share a little of ourselves with others, then the drawbridge goes up, and, because *the false self* is really an illusion – it has no real identity – these defences are often very high. It is essentially dualistic. *Me* and *not-me*, *inside* and *outside*, *friend* and *enemy*, *right* and *wrong*. In the dualistic mindset, reality, as we saw in the last chapter, is measured and controlled, not attended to, or met for what it really is. In Martin Buber's phrase, we continue to *measure* rather than *meet* reality.

Jesus comes to lead us out of this limited perspective. In the first instance, he doesn't have any problem with our weaknesses and frailties. We might fool others by our egocentric defence mechanisms, but we cannot fool God. Then the penny drops, that we don't have to fool God. He loves us and accepts every part of us, even, and especially, the unlovable bits that we want to hide. This is why he came. This is why he took on human form. This is what he offers: unconditional love and forgiveness. This is what he died for and in rising from the dead he offers this new possibility of Being to us. He calls this new life *the kingdom of God*. It is a new way of seeing, a new way of Being in the world, a new kind of consciousness.

Instead of looking out at other people, and the world, with the defensive egocentric mindset, we begin to see with another eye, the eye of the heart. It is a different operating system, a different kind of software. Where the mind is trapped in the binary system of dualism, the heart moves to a unified way of seeing and relating. This is not a descent into sentimentalism. It is not just about feelings. It is a different way of looking at everything. It moves us from a separate independent self to an awareness that our *true self* is always there in the centre of our being, in our souls; or, as many prefer to say, in our hearts. It unites us to the larger Being that vibrates in and enlivens the whole cosmos, and which we traditionally call God. It is a coming alive to this larger sense of *self*. It is becoming conscious of the flow of all life that connects everything together in a unified vision.

This new way of seeing is what Jesus is constantly talking about. In the middle of the Jewish Temple he stands up and cries out:

> Let anyone who is thirsty come to me and drink, and let the one who believes in me drink. As the scripture has said, *Out of the believer's heart shall come rivers of living water.*[41]

This new, living water will flow from the heart. He speaks of himself as light of the world. This new light changes everything:

> The lamp of the body is the eye. It follows that if your eye is sound, your whole body will be filled with light.[42]

This is the kingdom of God and Jesus says it is within. It is in the heart:

> Blessed are the pure in heart; they will see God.[43]

---

[41] Jn 7.37-39
[42] Mt 6:22
[43] Mt 5:8

Seeing with the eye of the heart doesn't neglect what we can learn with our rational minds, As I said in the last chapter, the higher levels of consciousness do not dismiss the lower levels; they include them in a deeper wisdom. The rational mind is a good, useful tool, but it is part of a larger, more inclusive way of seeing.

The dualistic mind always tends to make divisions, to make judgements, to divide the field. In the eye of the heart these divisions are not seen as primary. They are not denied; they are integrated at a deeper level. This is wisdom teaching. Jesus, for example, doesn't deny that we may have enemies. In saying that we have to love them rather than fight them, he is moving us to the wisdom of the heart. He moves to what unites us all – love – rather than what divides – suspicion and hate. Jesus is trying to move us to a non-dual level where all things and people can be reconciled.

Pragmatists might see this kind of love as naïve and impractical in the real world, a worthy dream, but not a realistic option. But we saw a famous dream become realised in the most powerful country on earth. The election of the first black president of the United States, Barack Obama, was an event that inspired people all over the world. In America it was described as the fulfilment of the dream so eloquently articulated by Martin Luther King, forty years ago in Washington. In the volumes of media comment on this dramatic event, I was struck by a text message circulated among the new president's supporters:

> Rosa sat, so that Martin could walk. Martin walked so that Barack could run. Barack is running so that our children can fly.

Rosa Parks was the brave black woman in Montgomery, Alabama, who refused to give up her seat on a bus to a white man. For this she was arrested and the subsequent Montgomery bus boycott triggered the whole civil rights movement led by Martin Luther King who adopted the policy of non-violence, first modelled, not by a Christian, but by Gandhi. Martin Luther King believed in love as the most transformative power not just in personal relationships, but in the wider political world.

This is not sentimental love; it is that deeper love that is called *agape*, a truly selfless love for others. It enabled King and his followers not only to endure the beatings, hosings and imprisonments that they suffered in those civil rights marches, but to transform that evil into love and forgiveness. As Martin Luther King put it:

> At this level we love the person who does an evil deed, although we hate the deed he does.

King is clearly speaking of a different level of consciousness that empowered him to look with the eye of the heart. His goal was not to defeat, but to try to change his enemy. At the time it might not have appeared to be successful, but over time his kind of reconciling love helped create the conditions that has given the United States its first black president.

I have suggested that there are two roads in our spiritual and human journey that bring about transformation. They are prayer and suffering. The African-American community of the United States has undergone suffering, from the years of slavery and discrimination, and all too recently in the events of Hurricane Katrina. Anything worthwhile in the struggle for human dignity that includes all people of every race, colour and creed has to be forged in the cradle of suffering. Our world seems forever poised on the axis of fear and love and it can tilt either way. Despite the past horrors of Rwanda once again we saw fighting breaking out in the Congo between Tutsi and Hutu. This is tribalism at its worst. I saw the same thing at first hand when I used to visit Liberia in the 1990s and the abuse of boy soldiers being forced to fight and kill in a largely tribal conflict. The violence in Iraq and Afghanistan continues, as does the mistrust and violence between Palestinian and Jew. Only yesterday, in our Asylum Link Centre here in Liverpool, I was listening to a young man relate his story of suffering from Darfur in the Sudan and a woman speaking of similar evils in Rwanda.

Those who are trapped at the egocentric levels of consciousness look at the world through the eyes of fear and mistrust. When you listen to leaders in any conflict the story is always the same: *It's their fault.* They talk like children in a playground fight: He hit me, so I am justified, in hitting him back. The only terrifying difference is that adult fighters are hitting back with ever more destructive weaponry. It is all about defending my tribe, my country, my point of view, my ideas, my religion. Nothing else is ever considered. The humanity of the enemy is screened out. The fact that my rival might have something to say is conveniently ignored. This is the poverty of dualistic thinking.

In the first axial age, referred to earlier, an increase in violence led to a counter-reaction when people moved to another level of awareness, to search for wisdom, and they forged the great religions of the world. Today we face even greater dangers as our weaponry, nuclear, biological, chemical and conventional, has reached appalling levels of destructiveness. At the same time our media technology has created a global village that we all inhabit. Our asylum centre in Liverpool welcomes men and women from all parts of Africa, from the Middle East and from the former Soviet Union. There is a great movement of people today and in the global village, where our world has become tribal, politics are no longer adequate. Humanity is being challenged to move to a different level of consciousness.

Four years ago I picked up a book in San Francisco that was written by Thomas Merton. It is called *Peace in the Post-Christian Era*. The book was intended for publication in 1962, but it was banned by the Abbot General of the Cistercian Order, Dom Gabriel Sortais. Merton was informed that this was not the kind of book a monk should be writing, because it falsified the monastic message. I don't wish to judge the Abbot General harshly, but his reaction illustrates the problems we all get into when we think dualistically: on the one hand there is prayer, on the other, the problems of the world.

The genius of Merton is that the more he prayed contemplatively the more deeply he became concerned about and involved in the problems of humanity. He understood that the old solutions were no longer working. This is what he wrote back in 1962:

> It should be clear from the moral and mental confusion of our time
> that the present world crisis is something far worse than a merely
> political or economic conflict. It goes far deeper than ideologies. It
> is a crisis of man's spirit. It is a completely moral upheaval of the
> human race that has lost its religious and cultural roots.[44]

Merton identifies the crisis as a spiritual crisis. Carl Jung used to say that the problems of most of his clients of mature years were, at root, spiritual. I think this is one reason why the Spirit of God is awakening us these days to the recovery of contemplative prayer, alongside the path of working for a more just world. These paths are not easy. They move us beyond comfort-zone religion with my ego still in control, to the discovery of *the true self*, which doesn't separate me from my brothers and sisters – it even includes my enemies – but uncovers our fundamental relationship and shared identity in God.

When the western monk, Thomas Merton, met the young eastern monk, Thich Nhat Hanh, in 1966 they discovered that they spoke the same language. They described each other as brothers. Together they brought the prayer life of their different traditions, Catholic and Buddhist, into a new kind of spirituality that best addresses the needs of our times. As in the first axial age, it is to be found in all the great religions of the world. It can be described as *engaged spirituality*.

---

[44] Thomas Merton *Peace in the Post-Christian Era* (Orbis Books, NY 2004) p127

It joins deep contemplative prayer to the search for a more socially just world. It is built on the insight that we cannot change others unless we change ourselves. We cannot force or compel others to change, as Christians sadly have too often done over the centuries. Our best contribution is to discover our true, common identity in God. This has long been the mystical insight and it is experienced when we make the journey within and learn to look out at the world with the eye of the heart.

Merton was not able to convince his Abbot General of the need to connect prayer with working for peace and the abolition of war. Nhat Hanh didn't succeed in convincing his fellow Vietnamese citizens of the need for change. He was exiled from Vietnam and still lives in exile today. Martin Luther King was shot dead. These men, and others, represent a new kind of hero for our times: the failed hero. In their lives we discern the pattern of the failed journey of Jesus who invited his people to see God in a new way, in the poor, in the rejected ones, in their enemies, and for this he was crucified. But in the divine plan the rejected one becomes the cornerstone of the new. The power of the Resurrection teaches us that nothing can be achieved without some kind of suffering, without some kind of failure. Suffering seems to be the best way to dismantle the defence mechanisms of the egocentric mind and its need for success and achievement.

This journey does not demand perfection. It recognises flaws and weaknesses and transforms them into a new creation. The eye of the heart is a compassionate, not a judging gaze, and it does this because it looks out from a heart that has been embraced and forgiven by a crucified God. The flawed hero knows that he is not perfect, that he is wounded. But he has made the difficult journey that all of us have to make. He has moved from a separate sense of existence to union with *ultimate reality*. He has abandoned the isolated, finite existence of *the false self* and moved into the spacious place where love is greater then fear. He glimpses the unity of all things. He is then able to teach that wisdom to others.

> The whole purpose of life is to restore to health the eye of the heart
> by which God may be seen.[45]

The day after Barack Obama was elected as President of the United States, I emailed a young Salesian Sister who is working with African-American children in the USA. Some of them are not well-motivated. I suggested that the election of a black president would help motivate these children to work harder at school and be less obstructive. She emailed back to say that sadly some of the kids had

---

[45] St Augustine *Sermon 88*

reacted wrongly to the election result. Their attitude was:

> We have the power now, we don't have to listen.

Many teachers and youth workers would be familiar with that kind of disappointing response from disadvantaged children. I have certainly experienced it myself in my teaching days. But our failure to create instant change has to be built into the long journey. We cannot always be successful, but we can be faithful. The journey goes on:

> Rosa sat, so that Martin could walk. Martin walked so that Barack could run. Barack is running so that our children can fly.

Chapter Seven
Why We Need Imperfection

Blessed are those who mourn for they will be
comforted.[46]

The problem with Jesus is that we think we know him and we know his story. I want to suggest that we can never really know Jesus in the sense that we know a friend or even a distant historical character. Jesus is a mystery and it is only the awareness that we are encountering a mystery that will save us from superficial and self-serving judgements. We say that Jesus is both human and divine and that immediately should warn us that this is no ordinary relationship. I would suggest Jesus is not just another person that we know in the sense that we sit in a room of friends, and there is Jesus sitting in the corner. When he calls himself, *The Way, The Truth and The Life*, he is telling us that knowing him is the truthful way to know everyone and everything else. It takes us to a different level of consciousness: from knowledge to wisdom and to love. This is what Paul means when he says that we live in Christ. We leave behind the calculating mind and learn to see with the eye of the heart.

Knowledge of Jesus unites two dimensions of the spiritual journey, the journey within and the journey without, the inner life of prayer and the outer life of action. He unites key dimensions of the Jewish tradition in his own person: he is a prophet, a mystic and a wisdom figure. Today I think it is the wisdom tradition that is coming to greater prominence in all the great religions. It teaches that the spiritual journey is about the transformation of the whole human being. This is the shift from *self-centred living* to *God-centred living*. We learn to live in and through compassionate love.

The gospels record Jesus asking the question to those who seek to follow him, *Who do you say I am?* He is trying to awaken the inner path to transformation. It is always a liberating encounter, and for those who are sufficiently aware, everything changes: the two disciples of John the Baptist respond to his invitation by leaving John's group to join Jesus. It is the same for the other apostles, who leave their nets, and everything else, to follow him. We sense it also in life-changing encounters as, for example, the Samaritan woman at the well. In this meeting we see how Jesus moves the woman through different levels of awareness so that she forgets the water in her bucket and asks him enthusiastically for the water of life:

> Sir, give me this water, so that I may never be thirsty or have to
> keep coming here to draw water.[47]

She tells him that she knows that The Messiah will come to teach all things. In response Jesus, for the first time in the gospel, reveals his true identity.

---

[47] Jn. 4:15

I am he, the one who is speaking to you.

When the apostles appear on the scene they are astonished at what is taking place, a meeting of real intimacy and mutuality between Jesus and this woman, who has a rather colourful past. She returns home transformed into an apostle and manages to bring other Samaritans to faith in him. Her words, *He told me everything I have ever done,* underline how Jesus transforms. He doesn't condemn or attack her past behaviour; he forgives it and transforms it.

This encounter underlines what I was saying about levels of awareness. The image of God is located in the heart's knowing. It is seeing with the eye of the heart. Jesus awakens the divine image, the divine energy in the heart of this woman, as he tries to do with everyone he meets. Not everyone is open to this level of encounter and Jesus weeps over the city of Jerusalem as the symbol of those who were too afraid, or too trapped in their own egos to open up to the challenge of transformation and liberation. But to return to the Samaritan woman, I want to highlight her past: the fact that she had five husbands and had been living a far from perfect and religiously correct life. Yet it is to this morally flawed woman that Jesus first reveals himself as the Messiah, echoing the great *I am* revelation to Moses. He doesn't condemn her for immorality; he places the narrative of her life in a wider context. He sees her true self.

What this teaches us is the critical importance of imperfection in understanding who God is. Imperfection is not something that we have to marginalize or try to hide, or excuse, but, in Richard Rohr's insightful phrase, *it is the organising principle of the way to God*. It is the framework inside which God makes himself known and calls us into union. The path into intimacy with God is through the wound, the tragic flaw, as described in all great Shakespearean and Greek theatre. Most of us, schooled in western individualism, still see the religious question as a personal struggle to try to get it right. We want to feel good about our moral and religious reputation. Yet the way that Jesus teaches is the very opposite. The wisdom of God is uncovered in human woundedness.

This is a severe challenge to our normal western default mode of fixing things and changing things. It is really up to us to get others on the straight and narrow path. Here again we meet the dualistic mindset. I'm basically OK, but I'm not too sure about various other people, so I have to sort them out. And the fact that I am doing it for God makes me feel even better and genuinely holy. In contrast, Jesus is a healer not a fixer.

Fixing is an act of the will; it is a confirmation of my strength and your weakness. It reinforces my sense of superiority. Healing is about mutuality; for Jesus, it is relational. When he heals, he is drawing out the inherent goodness in the other which may be obscured by woundedness and imperfection but is none the less there. He doesn't overwhelm anyone with his power, but empties himself and appears as a vulnerable human being, who can be rejected and misunderstood.

He comes to us as the one who refuses any kind of egocentric power. This is captured in St Paul's extraordinary passage in his letter to the Philippians. For Paul, this is the mind of Christ and this is what happens to us when we undergo the *metanoia* Jesus asks for:

> Let the same mind be in you that was in Christ Jesus
> who though he was in the form of God
> did not regard equality with God as something to be exploited, but
> emptied himself
> taking the form of a slave,
> being born in human likeness.
> And being found in human form,
> He humbled himself
> and became obedient to the point of death
> – even on a cross.
> Therefore God also highly exalted him
> and gave him the name
> that is above every name,
> so that at the name of Jesus
> every knee should bend
> in heaven and on earth and under the earth
> and every tongue should confess
> that Jesus is the Lord
> to the glory of God the Father.[48]

Paul uses the Greek word *kenosis* which means *to empty oneself,* or *to let go*. In this beautiful hymn, Paul is pointing to the software that Jesus constantly uses. He empties himself of Godhead to assume human form, and his whole life can be summed up as self-giving love for others. His life was not one of glorification, of achievement, of success, but of descent into vulnerability and apparent failure. On the cross, his naked, bleeding body becomes an icon of woundedness and powerlessness. Most of us, I think, pass over this passage in Paul, because we really don't want to go there.

---

[48] Ph 2:5-11

If we look at the history of Christianity, we have tended to promote the upward path. Since the emperor Constantine made Christianity the official Church of the Empire, we have built up and enjoyed positions of power and influence. Look at the hierarchy of the Church with its titles of *My Lord, Bishop, Monsignor, Your Eminence, Your Grace,* and even, *Your Holiness.* It is difficult to set all these and many other official titles and the opulent robes of office, with the poor man of Nazareth. It is easy to be critical and, if we are really honest, we all want to be on the spiritual ladder of success and enjoy a good reputation.

We prefer the religion of performance because it keeps our ego in charge. Even though we experience the longing for union for which God has created us, we allow that longing to be diverted into other less-loving kinds of behaviour. Our deepest desire is for wholeness and fulfilment; at root, it is the longing to be loved. However, something inevitably goes wrong and our search for love gets diverted into the pursuit of other things that we, really deep down, don't want, yet seem unable to resist. Rather than go down the path of self-emptying as Jesus does, we fill ourselves up with other desires. This is what Gerald May calls the problem of addiction.[49] We tend to think about addiction in terms of alcohol-abuse or drugs or sex, but in reality there are many forms of addictive behaviour. For Gerald May, it affects all of us in one way or other. It includes addictions to work, relationships, moods, power and control.

We can be enslaved to any of these addictions which produce compulsive behaviour patterns and reduce our desire for God. In our traditional theological language, we used the expression original sin, but the word sin tends to be interpreted in terms of personal guilt and culpability. What we are talking about in addiction is the wound at the heart of the human condition. Everyone shares this to some degree. It is the human wound.

Spiritual teachers are coming to the conclusion that the core addiction is to our own egocentric mind, our own thought processes that remain locked into dualistic patterns. It is the mind that keeps us trapped in lower levels of consciousness. What happens is that my desire to feel good about myself will not admit my own woundedness. We all experience this pain in some form or other. The unconscious mind seeks to push it onto someone else, or some other group, tribe or nation. I watched a BBC interview with the leader of the Tutsi army invading the eastern Congo, killing the Hutus in a tragic reverse of the original Rwanda war. The Tutsi leader came across as well-educated, intelligent and reasonable, but he was clearly still at the dualistic level of consciousness.

---

[49] Gerald May *Addiction & Grace* (Harper San Francisco 1991)

This was particularly the case when the reporter confronted him with evidence that his forces had killed innocent civilians. Like so many military commanders he simply denied that his men would ever do such a thing. Intelligent, *yes*; wise, *no*. Yet again the shadow is denied. When we look at the gospels, Jesus had no problem with sinners; his struggle was with those who denied that they were sinners.

Have you ever wondered why it is that Jesus spends so much time casting out devils, healing people who are described as possessed by demons? Modern liberal believers are a bit embarrassed by that kind of language, but in his recent best selling book, *The Power of Now*, Eckhart Tolle describes what he calls the pain body. We remember past hurts and every emotional pain we suffer in life gets stored in the mind and the body. They are stored in the unconscious and, if not dealt with, what happens is that instead of controlling my emotions, the emotions control me. This really is a kind of possession, and it accounts for so much of the anger, rage and violence we see in our families and society, and in so many conflicts across the world. In recent years we have seen the growth of road rage as a classic example. In our town centres, we see the outbreak of violence after a night's drinking. In wars, we see the torture and abuse of prisoners. In the war in the Congo, soldiers were taking out their anger on women who were victims of rape. But religious believers are not exempt from this repressed anger, as we find in many church groups and in religious communities. I recall being shocked a few years ago, when a Benedictine Retreat preacher said that, in his opinion, many religious communities run on aggression.

Tolle suggests that if we are to try to heal the *pain body* in the world we have to observe it first in ourselves. Pay attention to your moods, and ask yourself what is causing you unhappiness, irritation, impatience, anger or resentment. This kind of pain will look for something to feed on either within ourselves or in others. It feeds off energy and this energy takes the form of feeling victimised or looking for someone else to blame. Today we live in a culture that actively promotes the cult of the victim and constantly looks for scapegoats. Once I can identify myself as a victim, all I need is someone to blame. For some people, the question of pain becomes the software of their lives. It becomes the identity badge of *the false self*. We can even enjoy this kind of suffering. It keeps my world-view centred on myself and my needs. It finds expression in phrases like, *I have a right to do this or to get that, how could they do this to me? I deserve this, etc.*

How do we deal with this? Once you can bring this pain into consciousness, you lessen its intensity. By becoming aware and present to the pain you take away some of its sting. You become the witness or the watcher; now it is no longer controlling you unconsciously. This is bringing it into the light of consciousness. It is what Jesus speaks of when he takes on the forces of darkness symbolised by demonic possession. The light of healing grace takes away some of the addictive strength of the wound. It is not a case of fighting the pain because that would only give it more oppositional energy, and that is exactly what it is looking for. It is a case of becoming aware of it, becoming conscious. In the gospel you can see why the demons shouted at Jesus; he was so in tune with the light of *God consciousness*, that they sensed he would take away their power of possession, and he did exactly that.

Whenever you become aware of whatever is causing you pain recognise it as the *pain body* working in you. The key is not to cling to it, not to judge it or try to analyse it. The practice of contemplative prayer is so useful here, because in your practice you will have learned what to do with intrusive thoughts in moments of prayer. What matters is that you neither accept them nor reject them violently. Simply notice them, name them and then let them gently go by. It is the same with painful emotions, which are nothing other than thoughts. Wordless prayer is God's therapy for our wounded selves. Even when we feel nothing is happening in prayer, the Spirit works on our unconscious. We begin to experience a more forgiving and accepting love, for ourselves and for others.

Spiritual teachers encourage us to move from judgement, from analysis, from anger, from fear, to a new level of compassionate acceptance and forgiveness. We learn the meaning of the wisdom saying, *It is as it is.* This kind of wisdom embraces everything and transforms even the most difficult and challenging situations. When Jesus confronts the demons of possession, he treats the victims with great compassion. He touches them, he brings them back into the community, he reminds them of their true selves.

This is not easy, and it requires the distancing of ourselves from our egos. The ego has a strange fixation with pain. It wants that victim identity. For many people this is the only identity they have, so the ego will resist any attempt to undermine its control. We enjoy being the victim; it gives us a sense of power over the perpetrator. As Tolle says, we prefer to enjoy the *pain body* rather than let go of the hurt. It feeds the defensive mechanisms of the egocentric mind, which needs enemies to prop up its own false identity. The ego lives off fear and maybe that is why the most common one-liner, in the whole of the Jewish-Christian scriptures is, *Do not be afraid.*

This is why contemplative prayer is so important. It teaches me that I cannot escape this kind of possession on my own. It takes me down to confront all my fears and to empty myself of all these illusions that are giving life and energy to *the false self*. Contemplative prayer takes us down to that place deep in the soul where we experience our deepest fear which is the fear of unworthiness, of not being good enough, the fear of my own imperfection, the fear of failure; it is the hole in the soul. Without some kind of healing at this level people try to fill this hole in all manner of ways.

> So they strive after possessions, money success, power, recognition, or a special relationship, basically so that they can feel better about themselves, feel more complete. But even when they attain all these things, they soon find that the hole is still there, that it is bottomless.[50]

The situation might appear hopeless, but it is precisely at this point that the spiritual journey really begins.

The first thing we have to do, as we see in the quotation at the head of the chapter, is not to fight this wound but to accept it, to own it and to weep over it. This is very counter-intuitive for many Christians, especially men, who have been trained in the spirituality of success and achievement. But in the beatitude, Jesus suggests that to weep in this way is a profound spiritual moment. It literally breaks open our rather hardened hearts and opens them up to vulnerability, to powerlessness, to the self-emptying path of Jesus. At this deepest level of soul, we encounter the forgiveness and mercy of God. That is why imperfection is the way into spiritual transformation. This is the transforming path of Jesus, through death – of the false egocentric self – into the fullness of life, *the true self*. Eckhart Tolle makes the same point when he says:

> The secret of life is to *die death before you die* and find there is no death.[51]

This is why Jesus describes the state of mourning as *blessed*. He commends those who weep, those who are not afraid of their own pain. They are the ones who can carry the pain of the world. An asylum seeker once told me how much strength she drew from a Religious Sister working at the Refugee Centre. What did this sister do? *When I cry, she cries with me.* This weeping mode enables us to carry the dark side of human history and how to carry the pain of the world

[50] Eckhart Tolle *The Power Of Now* (Hodder & Stoughton London 2001) p 37
[51] Eckhart Tolle p 38

without looking for perpetrators or victims. It teaches us how to recognise the tragic flaw in human existence. It teaches us that life is imperfect and that is OK. It moves us beyond the ego's desire to split, to divide the world into good and bad, winners and losers. When we embrace non-dual thinking we see tears as tears: Palestinian, Israeli, Iraqi, Iranian, American, Somalian, British, Russian, it is all the same.

At the end of the infancy narrative, that has proclaimed the joyous birth of Jesus, Matthew concludes with the shocking slaughter of innocent children by Herod:

> A voice was heard in Ramah, wailing and loud lamentation, Rachel weeping for her children.[52]

This tragic event signifies that even with the coming of the Messiah, the dark side of human existence is not wiped out. Many other Rachels weep across our world today, and there needs to be a Rachel in our own hearts that can mourn our own pain.

In the wisdom and paradox of this beatitude, maybe Jesus is telling us something sacred about the human condition. That our woundedness and tragic flaws don't destroy us but in fact become the alchemy that transforms us and leads us into the compassionate, forgiving heart of God. When we can stop dividing good and evil, and learn to absorb it into our own souls then we can do what Jesus does on the cross when he reaches out both arms to embrace both the good and the bad thief.

It all comes down to the question of identity – *Who Am I?* Once we touch *the true self* in prayer we are, in a very real sense, indestructible. We begin to live a life that is larger than our own. We escape the trap of separate existence and move into the spaciousness of Being. But we can't get there by willpower, because that would be another ego achievement. We get there by letting go of our need for success and embracing our weakness. That is why many people give up contemplative prayer as useless. Nothing seems to be happening; we experience the poverty of the human condition. We cannot stop the flow of addictive thought-patterns. Here we learn that we cannot resolve our human woundedness by willpower. We have to open ourselves, in a receptive stance, before the grace of God.

This is the journey Paul famously described. After relating his mystical experience of being swept up to heaven, he is brought back to earth with a bump:

---

[52] Mt 2:18

To keep me from being too elated, a thorn was given to me in the flesh, a messenger of Satan to torment me. Three times I appealed to the Lord about this, that it would leave me, but he said to me, *My grace is sufficient for you, for power is made perfect in weakness.*[53]

Paul is so taken by this that he now boasts of his weakness, so that God's grace and power can be seen to be at work in him. This is death to the *ego*, and life in *the true self*. The grace of the Spirit given to us objectively at Baptism needs to grow and unfold in the struggles of our lives. Nothing apparently accelerates this growth as much as wounds that are accepted and mourned over. Once we have been humbled, God-consciousness can break in.

---

[53] 2 Cor. 12 7-9

THE COINCIDENCE OF OPPOSITES

Chapter Eight
The Coincidence of Opposites

In the west, the coincidence of opposites is
associated with the fifteenth century German
theologian, Nicholas of Cusa, who spoke of *learned
ignorance*. But I see it in all the mystics, and all
through the Bible it is a principle of Christian
living.[54]

---

[54] William Johnston *Mystical Journey: An Autobiography* (Orbis Books USA 2006) p 154

Prior to the Second Vatican Council, spirituality was dominated by the idea of self-denial. The idea was that the more difficult the action, the more painful and self-sacrificing, the more God would like it. I have talked to numerous religious over the years in my Retreat Ministry and heard endless stories of that ilk. Confronted by two choices of action, the inference always seemed to be that God would prefer the less congenial of the two. At worst, this led to some quite inhuman decisions. Some religious, for example, especially Sisters, were refused permission to visit dying parents or attend funerals. It was a self-denying and largely negative spirituality. It suggested that God likes to see us suffer.

After all those years of negativity it was no surprise to see a significant change after the Second Vatican Council. The dignity of the human person was restored in the conciliar documents and spirituality caught the mood, switching the emphasis from self-denial to self-fulfilment as the human sciences were embraced. Many traditional Catholics were puzzled by the abandonment of identity badges such as *No meat on Fridays*. Under the influence of psychology, the emphasis shifted to personal growth. Self-denial was replaced by self-fulfilment. While psychology can assist spirituality, it cannot replace it, because it doesn't go deep enough. What the gospels seem to demand from us is neither self-denial nor self-fulfilment, but a transformation of consciousness, a self-transcendence. The problem with both self-denial and self-fulfilment is that they both keep *the false self* intact, because it is me that is doing it. But the paradox of the spiritual life is that we cannot transform ourselves. It cannot be achieved by will-power.

The paradox, at the heart of mature spirituality, is the coincidence of opposites, a phrase that goes back to St Bonaventure. As we saw in the last chapter, there is no spiritual growth without embracing both light and dark. It is only when we experience the wisdom of the wound that transformation begins to happen. It is only when we enter into our poverty and emptiness that we can be filled with God. This is essentially the journey of contemplative prayer. The journey takes us away from achievement, fixing and controlling, and invites us to surrender to the mystery. The rational mind alone cannot grasp this paradoxical truth, but it was beautifully expressed by Jesus as the first of his beatitudes when he said:

Blessed are the poor in spirit, for theirs is the kingdom of heaven.[55]

In proclaiming the kingdom of God, Jesus invited his followers into this new consciousness, which can hold the opposites together. He taught that poverty was fullness, that meekness inherits everything, that gentleness is true strength.

---

[55] Mt 5:3

As we recover the tradition of contemplative prayer we are beginning to see what the Buddhists have consistently taught about possessions. It doesn't differ from the apophatic[56] tradition of the Christian mystics. Total emptiness is total fullness. Jesus calls this a blessed state. It completely undermines and contradicts what the western world has taught about possessions. Again, we have to be careful. It doesn't mean that material things are bad; it is in the clinging to them and the attachment to them that the problems arise. That is why Matthew's version of the beatitude differs from Luke, who simply says *Blessed are the poor*. Matthew adds the words *poor in spirit*. It is possible to be materially poor and still very unaware of kingdom values, living from a very different consciousness.

But it is also possible to be a religious believer, regular churchgoer, without any real transformation taking place. I think what Jesus, and Paul, in his great hymn to the self-emptying of Jesus, are pointing towards, is the recognition that the self alone, the ego alone, cannot experience transformation. When Jesus was completely emptied out, he saved the world. On the cross, in complete defeat, his saving power is fully expressed. The rational mind can never really explain this mystery.

The beatitudes are rooted in the coincidence of opposites. Before Jesus teaches about the need to create a just world he takes us to a deeper space, a different kind of awareness, which demands a surrendering of the ego. He speaks of poverty, of gentleness, of mourning, all summed up in a new way of seeing which Jesus calls purity of heart. We have tended to interpret this as referring to the virtue of chastity, but I think it best sums up Jesus' teaching about seeing from the eye of the heart. This kind of seeing can hold opposites together and allow something new to emerge. Each beatitude does this and it contradicts the logical, rational mind. The secular mind – and I think many Christians also if we are honest – see this kind of teaching as worthy but not very practical in the real world. Building a world of social justice calls for very vigorous action, for a confrontation with evil and with the perpetrators of evil. Gentleness, poverty and mourning suggest rather pious weakness. What Jesus is saying makes nice poetry but it won't change the world.

In fact, Jesus is trying to be eminently practical but, until we change our awareness and consciousness, we will not be able to understand. Many people work for social justice in our world, but all too often they want to change the world, while keeping the ego intact. Almost every great revolution in history demonstrates that without a change of consciousness, without real inner work, all that happens is that one set of oppressors is replaced by another. The Communist revolution dramatically illustrates how you cannot change external reality without some inner change.

---

[56] See page 30.

When Jesus speaks about the kingdom mentality, he is taking us to that level of awareness when we move beyond the dualistic split of good and evil, to a deeper space, a space emptied of my egocentric judgements. Here I can learn to embrace all things, to taste the underlying unity that sees the divine image in all people. It requires a non-dual looking at all things. It demands a contemplative gaze that looks without judgement, without analysis. This is the work of contemplation.

We have to immediately qualify that statement and recognise the paradox again: we cannot do this for ourselves. Many of the great saints have been quoted as teaching the important truth that we have to pray as if everything depends on God, and work as if everything depends on us. We are beginning to understand again today why every religious founder insisted on the vow of poverty at the heart of religious life. While this demands some concrete manifestation in the way religious live in solidarity with the poor, at the same time it invites us to make the much more difficult task of emptying ourselves of our dearest possession, our ego. Maybe one of the reasons for the decline of religious vocations may be because people no longer see many religious prepared to do this. I know how difficult I find this in my own experience.

The coincidence of opposites leads all of us in the Church today, out of comfort-zone religion into the transformation of consciousness. After the Second Vatican Council, many Catholics took up the issues of justice and peace. This is clearly a good thing, but we are realising now that justice-building demands a completely different way of reading reality and taking-in reality. At the centre of this is the movement from the small egocentric sense of self to the larger sense of *the true self*. This can only happen when we adopt those challenging words of Jesus in the beatitudes. In fact, the small self simply cannot create justice as an ego game, because the ego will always want to retain a sense of superiority. I remember a group of religious in Ireland a few years ago writing to the Taoiseach (Prime Minister) about the need to protect and defend the poor in the government's up-coming budget. At that time leaders of religious orders were described as *major religious superiors*. He was a clever politician and he replied that he wasn't prepared to listen to any concerns about the poor from a group that signed itself as *major* and *superior*. I'm sure that the leaders of religious communities are humble men and women, but after that riposte they subsequently changed their group-name.

Postmodern people are put off by critique, denouncements and analysis that seems to come from above. The world has grown very critical of external authority that doesn't appear to be backed up by the authority of some inner experience. While being quick to point out the faults and failings of others over the years, especially in the area of sexual morality, too many Church leaders were slow to react to the problems raised by the sexual abuse crisis. We all need to have the highest ideals put before us, but in a complex world moral teaching and preaching needs a lot of humility and honesty. None of us are perfect and we don't live in a perfect world.

Contemplative prayer provides a healing space where we can meet and embrace the coincidence of opposites. The cross of Christ teaches us that reality is not perfect but cruciform. This is the pattern of all reality. We are told in the letter to the Ephesians that the plan of God is for Christ to bring all things together in unity. In this book I have been trying to suggest that all things are one, the problem is that our egocentric minds give us a different message. What the coincidence of opposites can do is to provide a larger space where we can overcome the dualisms and bring them to a deeper unity. In becoming incarnate Jesus agreed to enter a mixed world of good and bad, of light and dark, of joy and sorrow. Our world is both blessed and broken, *at the same time*. As we saw in the previous chapter, with the wisdom of the wound we have to learn to reach out to others and include them in the kingdom of God. This can only happen if we go deeply into the place in our souls where we experience our own divisions and splits.

Our rational minds cannot avoid the problem of splitting. We are caught between subject and object. In analysing and judging, our minds keep us trapped in this split consciousness. That is why Jesus so often uses a child as the visual aid for a different kind of awareness. A child is still open to the unity at the heart of all things. Some teachers call this attitude, *beginner's mind*. Jesus says that unless we return to that we cannot enter the kingdom. That is why he tells us to go into that secret place to pray, and not to use too many words. Instead of looking at reality and judging it, or naming it, we simply learn to look. The subject/object split then disappears and we become one with everything. Everything is seen for what it is: pure being. There is no judgement or labelling. There is just the moment.

The experience of the present moment, which is at the heart of wordless prayer, cannot be put into words. It cannot really be reflected upon because that is to go back into the subject/object awareness. In the moment of loving attention, there is nothing to defend. Such an awareness cannot be achieved, it is not the result of effort. It has to be received. If we drift off to other thoughts, we can gently use the sacred word to return to loving attention. The sacred word is about consent not effort.

This kind of awareness is usually experienced in self-emptying. In that moment of poverty and emptiness we begin to experience everything as a gift. It is no particular place; Thomas Merton calls it the *palace of nowhere*. Centering prayer places us there, in an attitude of complete abandonment. There is no space for judgement, for critique, for analysis.

Everything is one. It is a moment without past or future. It simply is. During these moments, the Holy Spirit can slowly transform us so that when we return to normal consciousness, the coincidence of opposites no longer makes us angry or alienated. It is what it is. This doesn't mean that life is a bed of roses, or that we can avoid the struggle for justice. The paschal mystery of Jesus teaches us that we will experience both pain and sorrow. Instead of pushing the pain of life away from us, or blaming others, we will be able to transform it within our own souls.

Some activists might argue that this is simply drawing back from the struggle for justice in an unjust world. I don't think this is true. There is no doubt that Jesus makes a clear option for the poor in his ministry. Indeed he defined his mission precisely in those terms:

> The Spirit of the Lord is upon me, because he has anointed me to bring good news to the poor. He has sent me to proclaim release to the captives and recovery of sight to the blind, to let the oppressed go free, to proclaim the year of the Lord's favour.[57]

Jesus sees his work of liberation of the poor and suffering as the work of the Spirit in which he is totally absorbed. It is relational work. He reaches out to include those who feel excluded. His task is not to punish those who cause injustice, but rather to move them beyond their egocentric judgements and maltreatment of others into true relationship, to discover *the true self* hidden within. That is why he calls his followers to work for justice in the right relational spirit, not out of anger or seeking to punish others. In the eyes of Jesus, those who create and maintain injustices are also victims.

Matthew's gospel brilliantly underlines two different approaches between Jesus and John the Baptist. Chapter 11 records the incident when John, who has been imprisoned by Herod, seems to be having real doubts about Jesus. He sends his disciples to Jesus to ask:

> Are you the one who is to come or are we to wait for another? Jesus answered them, Go and tell John what you hear and see: the blind receive their sight, the lame walk, the lepers are cleansed, the deaf hear, the dead are raised, and the poor have the good news brought to them.[58]

---

[57] Lk 4:18-19
[58] Mt 11:2-5

And then he adds a curious phrase:

> And blessed is anyone who takes no offence at me.[59]

Jesus seems to be well aware of the challenging nature of what he is doing. He continues in the typical style of a wisdom teacher to make a paradoxical statement about John. He declares that of all the children born of women, there has never been anyone greater than John the Baptist; but in the very same sentence he says:

> The least in the kingdom of heaven is greater than he.[60]

He seems to be suggesting that the kingdom provides a higher form of consciousness than even John demonstrated. What does he mean by this?

If you look at John's preaching in Chapter 3 of Matthew's gospel it has a hard edge to it. John gives a kind of job description for the coming Messiah:

> Even now the axe is lying at the root of the trees; every tree therefore, that does not bear good fruit is cut down and thrown into the fire.[61]

> His winnowing-fork is in his hand, and he will clear his threshing floor, and will gather his wheat into the granary; but the chaff he will burn with unquenchable fire.[62]

When John's disciples visit him in prison their reports of Jesus' ministry must have disappointed him, hence the doubt recorded in his question. In his reply to John, Jesus reveals that his mission is about forgiveness and inclusion, not punishment. The healing miracles he alludes to, reveal a different kind of God, one that requires a new form of seeing: the blind see; a new way of hearing: the deaf hear; a new sense of human dignity: the lame walk. There is no talk of scattering the chaff and cutting down trees to throw into the fire. It appears that for all his courage and bravery John seems locked into the *conditional* love of God, who will reward the good and punish the bad. Jesus, on the other hand, reveals the *unconditional* love of his Father whose sun rises on the good and the bad and whose rain falls on the just and the unjust. That is the new consciousness of the kingdom that is clearly on the side of the poor, and wants us to read reality from the viewpoint of the poor, but at the same time is offering forgiveness and reconciliation to those responsible for the world's injustices.

---

[59] Mt 11:6
[60] Mt 11:11
[61] Mt 3:10
[62] Mt 3:12

Rather than being a position of weakness, this ability to hold the opposites together is what will bring about true peace and reconciliation in our very violent world. It demands an enormous amount of courage and vision, and it doesn't come easily. The practice of contemplative prayer is a sure foundation where this level of awareness can grow. Not everyone learns it this way. For many of the poor it is simply how they respond to the injustices inflicted upon them. I am constantly amazed by the patience and the cheerfulness – in the midst of much pain and suffering – exhibited by the asylum seekers I meet. Prayer and suffering seem to be the two best ways to dismantle our egos.

A few years ago, I was visiting Hong Kong to observe the Salesian work there. An English Salesian priest had set up a very impressive programme for homeless young people at risk from Triad gangs and drug dealers. While there, the Provincial took us to visit a community of elderly Salesians, where I met two remarkable priests. They had been imprisoned by the Chinese communists for twenty-seven years. During that time, they had been badly treated and their daily circumstances were extremely challenging. They had no contact with any other Salesians, or with any members of their families or friends. They could not celebrate Mass, or keep any religious possessions such as a breviary, a crucifix, a holy picture, or rosary beads. One of them was now in a wheelchair, his back having been badly damaged working in labour camps for so many years. What really impressed me about these two priests was their serenity, their simple joy. There was no sign of bitterness or anger or desire for revenge against those who had deprived them of the best years of their active ministry. They were truly grounded in God in a way that was quite evident. I don't think they would consider themselves as saints, but there was a greatness about them, and I have never forgotten it. They had reached that level of soul where they had discovered that, even in the most trying of circumstances, the ultimate reality is love.

Many Christians like to cling to the dogma and rituals that keep them in a safe comfort-zone. To live with the mystery of the coincidence of opposites is to accept the complexity of reality. Rather than embrace easy answers it leads us to taste life's dilemmas not with blind certainty, but with trust in the God who guides us with both the pillar of light and the pillar of cloud. Those who can live like this can truly help transform the world.

When Jesus proclaims that the poor, the gentle, those who mourn, and the pure in heart are blessed, I think this is what he means: they, more than anyone, have this ability to bring about transformation. Theirs is the kingdom, the new consciousness. They are blessed.

Chapter Nine

Contemplation and Action

If Christ became Man, it is because he wanted to
be any man and every man. If we believe in the
incarnation of the Son of God, there should be no
one on earth in whom we are not prepared to see,
in mystery, the presence of Christ.[63]

---

[63] Thomas Merton *New Seeds of Contemplation* (New Directions Paperbook NY 1972) p 296

Reading the classic writers on contemplation, you could get the impression that contemplative prayer is reserved for the few. Even Merton, who did more than anyone to rediscover the contemplative tradition, tends to frame his writings for a restricted audience, although he was open to the possibility that all people could access this gift. He was certainly interested in exploring the treasures of fellow contemplatives who were Zen Buddhists, Hindus and Moslem Sufis. What is so exciting about today is the fact that the Spirit seems to be prompting so many lay people as well as religious to explore what Jesus taught about silent prayer. The invitation to go into the private room, close the door and meet the Father, Son and Spirit in the secret of the heart is being taken up by more and more people.

A few months ago I preached a series of Retreats to my Salesian brothers in the Philippines. The closing Eucharist was held in the chapel-on-the-hill. It was an ideal place to conclude a Retreat. The stone floor of the chapel was marked by a labyrinth, which is an ancient symbol of the spiritual journey, one that is being rediscovered in Retreat houses around the world. A labyrinth is not a maze, but a carefully-constructed visual image of the inner and outer dimensions of the spiritual quest. It always leads into the centre, there the pilgrim is invited to stand and be receptive to whatever message the Spirit communicates to the heart. The inner journey is only half of the path; you then have to walk through the twists and turns of the outer journey. Both elements are necessary and remind us that the inner life and outer life are profoundly connected. Here again we meet and explore the coincidence of opposites.

At the moment, our world doesn't present a good balance between inner and outer. In the West we live in a profoundly extraverted culture. This is not just a secular problem; it exists also in the Church. Many priests and religious tend to put the emphasis on external action. If this is true for the clergy, then clearly the Christian formation of the laity is going to reflect that bias This is why, I think, the Spirit is speaking in the deepest recesses of our hearts. This imbalance is not new, as the mystics have long since told us. Despite so many technical advances, which would have been unimaginable to former generations, we all seem stressed by the pace of life today. We have never had so much entertainment available to us, yet I am not sure we are really that happy and at peace. I am a football fan. When I go to games and I see so many youngsters dressed in their expensive replica shirts, and their designer trainers, I think of the children I watched one Saturday afternoon in Liberia, West Africa, playing barefoot and in rags. I joined in the game with them. After some minutes, the ball split apart.

They tried to continue playing but it broke up in pieces. And yet there was laughter and a lot of fun as we played that game.

One of the good consequences of modern media is a new awareness of the disparities of wealth that exist in our world. We are much better informed about the injustices of our world. Many Christians feel inspired to help to improve the lot of the poor, both abroad and in our own countries. In fact, the problems are so evident that we tend to think that action is all that is needed. The idea of silent prayer, of an inner journey into the silence of the heart, appears to be of little practical use. The majority of Catholics are content to say their prayers, go to Mass, and want to be of service to their neighbour. Wordless prayer, frankly, seems a waste of time, a bit of a luxury. Given our deeply pragmatic culture, Christians are just as weighted towards external action as any ethical non-believer who wants to make the world a better place.

So why do we need an inner journey? I think it comes down to the quality of *presence* that we bring to our activity. In an earlier chapter I referred to *The Power of Now* by Eckhart Tolle. This book has become an international best seller. His message is that the only moment we have available to us is the *now*. We can no longer access the past and when the future arrives it will be experienced as the *now*. What matters is the attention and awareness we can bring to the *now*. This echoes traditional spiritual teaching about the sacrament of the present moment, or as Jean-Pierre de Caussade called it *Abandonment to Divine Providence*. De Caussade says that we can only find the will of God in this actual moment. Whatever is present now is the will of God. Everything is to be welcomed as the will of God. We have to learn to accept the things that we cannot avoid and endure things we don't like.

Despite being entertained and distracted by every kind of technical marvel: films, television, DVDs, MP3 players, computer games, the one phrase we seem to hear more than ever is *I am bored*. It seems that there is a restlessness and dissatisfaction in almost every experience. Spiritual teachers have long identified this restlessness with the desire that God has placed in all of us, for union with Him. Until we experience that union, our human hearts will never be satisfied.

> There is within us a fundamental disease, an unquenchable fire
> that renders us incapable, in this life, of ever coming to full peace.
> This desire lies at the centre of our lives, in the marrow of our
> bones and in the deep recesses of the soul.[64]

---

[64] Ronald Rolheiser *Seeking Spirituality* (Hodder & Stoughton London 1998) p 3

In many ways this is not what we want and our restlessness drives us to a myriad ways of satisfying our desires. We explore all kinds of blind alleys. This is the essence of all great art, music, and literature: the desire at the heart of the human spirit.

It is also the driving force behind the religious quest. But even in our religious searching we experience frustration. The sacrament of the present moment demonstrates that the moment is never as good as we would wish it to be. My own Salesian spirituality speaks about the sacrament of the ordinary. But the ordinary is ordinary. We don't spend many days on Mount Tabor, or at the side of a tranquil lake, or gazing at a beautiful sunset.

This is where those rather detached mystics, that we read about, are revealed as the most practical spiritual men and women. They teach us to move into the moment, to taste it fully, not to want to rush onto the next thing. They teach us to become aware, to be truly conscious. They teach us to *seek God as God is* and not *God as we would like him to be*. This is the essence of contemplative prayer. The mystery of the Incarnation is revealed in the fact that Jesus took on the ultimate poverty of the human condition.

We are all familiar with the visit of the wise men to the stable in Bethlehem, and the gifts that they brought. These gifts carry immense spiritual symbolism. The gift of frankincense is a symbol of prayer, and it is through that gift that the other two gifts are fully revealed. The gold represents the divine image in every human being. Myrrh, the bitter ointment, points to the darker side of life, the pain which is the other side of joy. Here again we have the mystical coincidence of opposites: the gift of prayer is the place where both gold and myrrh can be embraced and offered to God. We have to learn to live in an imperfect world. Everything in our lives, both gold and myrrh, can be used for transformation.

In the deepest part of our soul everything is seen as one. This is the essential insight that unites contemplation and action. It was this kind of transforming insight that Thomas Merton experienced in what has been called his Louisville vision. On a humdrum Saturday afternoon, as people went about their normal business, Merton saw the inner beauty of their souls. Having sought to separate himself from the world as a rather godless place and become a Trappist monk, he suddenly became aware of his love for and his deep unity with those people whom he did not know. They were no longer strangers. He described this shattering experience as waking from a dream of separateness. Merton saw separateness as the dream it really is. He now realised that the idea of living a separate holy existence was meaningless. After this profound experience of the real, this monk, who had been writing about the contemplative life, started to address the great social issues of his day. The years of silent prayer had led to the breakdown of his ego defences. Now he could truly see with a unified vision. He had become fully conscious.

This is why Jesus seems to put the inner journey before the outer journey especially in his concentrated teaching in the Sermon on the Mount. In his wisdom-teaching, Jesus promotes both the inner and the outer journey, but the emphasis on the inner journey warns us of the danger of the ego. The ego is very clever at disguising itself in action, even action on behalf of the poor.

> Woe to you scribes and pharisees, hypocrites! For you clean the outside of the cup and of the plate but inside they are full of greed and self-indulgence. You blind pharisee, first clean the inside of the cup so that the outside also may become clean.[65]

The inner journey clearly takes priority for Jesus. I know this is true in my own life. Too much success even in spiritual matters still feeds the ego. I have preached many Retreats and given talks, and sometimes I have looked at evaluations afterwards. Comments are often very favourable but sometimes they are not. It is amazing how that can affect my mood. I can even get quite angry at negative comments. That is my ego, which always wants to be liked by others and have a good reputation.

I think this is true in many of the things I think I am doing for God. I need to become more conscious of my mixed motives in trying to do good. This is not an easy lesson to learn, which is probably why I often shun the inner journey and prefer to get into action. Fixing and changing other people is much more attractive than facing my own mixed motives. Centering prayer, on the other hand, takes me to that deeper place where all can be held and accepted. Then I can move out into action. Without some kind of inner journey many people simply burn themselves out. In wordless prayer and presence I learn the vital lesson that success and failure doesn't depend on me. This is why some form of spiritual *practice* is essential. I have suggested contemplative prayer, but it can be any kind of practice: the rosary, going to Mass, whatever takes you back to that place of union where everything is one. And if your practice is making you judgemental of others, then find another practice!

The ego will always define itself with reference to others. It will do this by comparing, critiquing and judging. It always says *No* rather than *Yes*. It keeps

---

[65] Mt 23:25-26

reinforcing the walls of division and separation. While the movement of the ego is contraction, the movement of the soul, on the other hand, is expansion. It seeks inclusion not exclusion. I have to learn to trust that deepest part of myself that is the divine image in me, *the true self*. And that means trusting the deepest part of my own divine image. *The true self* is able to hold and contain *the false self*. It reminds me that original blessing comes before original sin. I have met so many people in different parts of the world who still feel bad about themselves. If I do not really like myself, then that is the self that I inflict on others in my work. It is a case of too much myrrh and not enough gold in our lives. In the inner work of prayer this imbalance can be rectified. In our extraverted culture this kind of inner work is more necessary than ever.

In our deepest souls the Holy Spirit can transform the negative judgements into positive ones. We have to make judgements in certain situations but they need to come from a place of peace, of love, and of union, not anger and jealousy. At the core of our being they are coming from a different consciousness. As we saw in Chapter Five, we move from measuring reality to meeting reality. Instead of trying to fit *the Other* into my preconceived ideas I can open up to the mystery and presence of God, even in people I dislike. Jesus is trying to take us there when he asks us to love and accept our enemies, because his Father allows his sun and rain to fall on them as he does on the just. Deepak Chopra suggests that these amazing words of Jesus reveal his true being and our being also:

> The clue lies in the two images he chose: the sun and the rain. These are the basis of life, the very sources of nourishment. Jesus is pointing us to our own source. There is a level of awareness inside everyone that is as steady as the sun and as life-giving as rain. This is pure Being, and without a connection to it, loving your enemy is impossible.[66]

Contemplative prayer provides the opportunity for the soul to expand by reaching out towards and including *the Other*.

A better balance between action and contemplation leads to better action. To act on behalf of others is necessary; *how* I act is even more important. If I can set aside my egocentric mind, my action will spring from a deeper place, one that seeks to include not exclude. My action will be truly on behalf of the kingdom and not my own self-promotion. I can become more fully present to the moment before me. Instead of trying to fix other people's lives I can learn to work with them and alongside them and I, too, can be changed for the better.

---

[66] Deepak Chopra *The Third Jesus* (Rider & Co 2008) p 56

In the Catholic Church, religious orders and congregations have traditionally highlighted the division between action and contemplation. While monks and cloistered nuns dedicated themselves to prayer other religious communities took a more active role, working in education and care for the sick. The saints who founded these active orders were all men and women of prayer, but some of their followers, because the needs were so great, were tempted to abandon prayer for activity. When my own founder, St John Bosco, was being canonised questions were raised. If he did so much work and achieved so much, did he really find time to pray? Don Philip Rinaldi, who became one his successors as Rector Major of the Salesians, gave personal testimony to the contemplative dimension of Don Bosco's life. At the beginning of 1931 he sent this message to the Salesian family:

> Don Bosco united in the most perfect way his tireless, absorbing, extensive, external activity, full of responsibility, with an interior life based on the presence of God, which little by little became habitual and led him to perfect union. In this way he brought about in himself the most perfect state, which is contemplation in activity, the ecstasy of action.[67]

The saints, like Don Bosco, knew that authentic action on behalf of the kingdom has to be rooted in a genuine prayer life. In article 12 of our Salesian rule of life we are called to be *contemplatives in action*. Today we are becoming more aware of the importance of this challenge.

The gospels tackle this issue in the Martha/Mary story.[68] While Mary sits at the feet of Jesus in a contemplative gaze, Martha is trying to prepare a meal. She is described as *distracted* by her many activities. Clearly there is nothing wrong with what she is doing: hospitality is very important; but it is the way in which she is doing it. *The false self* takes over in classic style: she starts to compare Mary's behaviour against hers. This comparison makes her angry and judgemental. She asks Jesus to tell her sister to help her. Jesus doesn't get angry with her; but he gently points out that she has become worried and distracted, both clear symptoms of *the false self*. He reminds her that only one thing is really necessary: to access *the true self* which desires nothing but union with God. Jesus says that Mary has chosen this and this will not be taken away from her.

I think what Jesus is trying to teach Mary – and all of us – is that contemplative prayer helps us to become truly present to God and therefore to everything

---

[67] Don Philip Rinaldi.
[68] Lk 10:38-42

else. Action is important, but it has to be rooted in this deep centre of the soul where we are in communion with God. Otherwise the ego will take over and we will get anxious and critical of others. Martha's remark, *tell my sister*, reveals the egocentric mind's desire to change someone else, but not to change myself. Mary would have heard the conversation between Jesus and Martha; and I would imagine that she would then get up to help her. Her action would be coming from a deeper source: love. The question of motivation is so important in our Christian lives and activity. Jesus doesn't seem too impressed by the volume of activity – Martha, anxious about many things – but he is very concerned about the quality of the presence.

This need to balance action and contemplation is further illustrated by the Franciscan, Richard Rohr[69] in highlighting two distinct yet complementary styles of literature in the scriptures. He compares and contrasts the prophetic with the apocalyptic. The prophets challenge all societies to practise more transformative action, especially on behalf of the poor. They call for repentance and conversion. In contrast, the apocalyptic style suggests that we can never overcome the world's corruption and achieve a just world. It calls for a more revolutionary stance. Rohr makes the point that these extremes need each other. It is another example of the coincidence of opposites.

The Church has tended to push its apocalyptic stance in the area of sexual morality. We preferred to be morally correct in this area rather than engage in the radical demands of true kingdom building. Compare the volume of teaching on sexual matters with the volume concerned with non-violent peacemaking. We could be seen to be radical without any real engagement with our enemies, or with the whole question of being successful or righteous.

The great Jewish prophets such as Isaiah, Jeremiah, Micah, Amos and Elijah were deeply concerned with the social agenda of their day. They suffered because of their courage and bravery in speaking God's word to the establishment. Many of them were killed, yet God continued to raise up more prophets to remind the people of the vital link between worship and the political decisions that shaped society. Some of the prophets such as Ezekiel and Daniel used the apocalyptic style, which appears similar to the prophetic but, in fact, seriously differs. Both John the Baptist and Jesus used this style and imagery and the Bible ends with John's book of Revelation, which Catholics called the Apocalypse.

---

[69] Richard Rohr and others *Grace in Action* (Crossroad NY 1994) pp 174 -177

The apocalyptic message differs from the prophetic in revealing that despite all the effort at building a better world by social engagement, we should never take ourselves too seriously. The emphasis is that the world belongs to God and we need to find a place in our souls where we can accept that. That might seem an easy way out, but it challenges the egocentric mind that thinks it can fix and change everything. Many people engage in social action only to experience burn-out, or to get angry and bitter. So, as Rohr points out, the need is to find a balance between the coincidences of opposites: everything matters and yet nothing matters. Thomas Merton is a striking example here, because when he moved into the domain of strong social criticism, at the same time he was living the life of a hermit. There was no mention of Merton engaging in protest marches like Martin Luther King, or going to prison over nuclear weapons like the Berrigan brothers. We need both vocations in the Church. We need to learn how to say *Yes* and *No*, to know when to act and when to cease from action, when to engage and when to enter the inner room.

As we saw earlier, both styles are represented in Jesus who contains the prophetic and the apocalyptic style of his ministry in his wisdom-teaching about a compassionate embrace of everything. He shows us how to put it all together. This will never be a popular position because, rather than take sides, it calls for holding both sides of the dilemma. Here reality can be seen as it truly is: neither wholly good nor wholly bad, but a cruciform mixture of both. And so are we.

Chapter Ten
Present to Mystery

Examine yourselves to see whether you are living
in the faith. Test yourselves. Do you not realise that
Jesus Christ is in you?[70]

The greatest misfortune that can befall you as a
Christian is not to know consciously that God lives
within you.[71]

---

[70] 2 Cor 13.5
[71] St Symeon, the new theologian, 10th Century

Writing this chapter, on Christmas Eve 2008, I am conscious of a wondrous event which happened exactly forty years ago. The Apollo 8 space mission to the moon in December 1968 went into lunar orbit on Christmas Eve. In the UK it was 3am on Christmas morning. Astronauts William Anders, Jim Lovell and Frank Borman witnessed something never seen before: from the moon, they saw the earthrise. The crew got their cameras and took those iconic colour pictures of planet earth. The earth appeared as a tiny planet of blue, green and brown hanging in the blackness of space. As the astronauts orbited round the back of the moon they lost radio contact with Houston mission control. When they re-established communication William Anders began to read: *In the beginning God created the heaven and the earth. And the earth was without form, and void; and darkness was on the face of the deep.* One by one, these highly trained technicians read the opening paragraphs of the book of Genesis. Borman concluded with the words, *and God saw that it was good. And we close with good night, good luck, a merry Christmas – and God bless all of you on the good earth.* Like the astronauts quoted in the first chapter these men had been profoundly moved and sought the language of mysticism and spirituality to describe what they were experiencing. They had become present to mystery.

The astronauts experience was special and extraordinary, but the mystical tradition of all religions testifies that such experiences can become normal. It demands a disciplined and regular commitment to a time for prayer, to meditation, and to silence, but everything in our culture militates against this. The Dalai Lama was once reduced to tears by an American audience, when he was asked how they could become instantly enlightened. We expect everything to happen quickly and we have become addicted to noise and endless stimulation. We are an over-stimulated culture. Just think of the number of images you will have seen from the media in the course of a lifetime. It is not easy to detach from this.

We have seen how the Church recognises two styles of prayer. The cataphatic tradition uses words, images and music. The apophatic tradition, on the other hand, goes beyond words and images, into silence. This tradition taught that ultimately everything we say about God can only be a metaphor. Of course, we need a balance of both traditions, of knowing and unknowing, but there is a growing awareness in our extraverted culture of a need to redress the balance and give more time to the apophatic tradition. This imbalance has existed for almost four hundred years, as we saw in chapter two. During that period we thought we could know everything through our rational, logical minds. We reduced everything to our thinking minds. Our doctrines and dogmas tried to put everything into words, and we even had a pocket version of all this in the catechism. Catholics thought they were on top; they had all the answers. Not surprisingly the tradition of not knowing was sidelined and almost forgotten. Protestants, too, neglected this tradition as we fought our theological battles over words and definitions.

We have started to lose our presence to the mystery. The rediscovery of the apophatic tradition today is a response to a real hunger in our souls. This kind of spirituality searches for the God *behind and within the mystery*; for the invisible, beyond and within the visible. It points bravely to the emptiness at the heart of everything; an emptiness that both mystics and quantum scientists are saying contains everything. This is difficult for the western rational mind, which restricts our awareness to knowledge and facts and data. But our studies of the mind today reveal its bi-polar structure. We have long been dominated by our left-brain thinking, emphasising logic and reason. For too long we have neglected the right brain which embraces art, symbols, poetry, paradox and ambiguity. This is the crossover point in our consciousness, noted in chapter five, inviting us beyond measuring reality, to meeting it. Such wisdom takes our facts, information and data and places them inside a bigger picture. The Old Testament called this bigger picture *the Promised Land*, and Jesus called it *the Kingdom of God*. It is a new kind of consciousness, a new way of looking at reality, beyond the egocentric mind.

After beginning his public ministry with the invitation to enter this new consciousness (metanoia), Jesus went into the desert for forty days to show us how to do this. The wilderness is a classic place of understimulation; it is a place of unlearning and unknowing. Jesus was teaching us how to get beyond the egocentric, judging mind. He clearly wasn't saying *Our Fathers* and *Hail Marys*; he was teaching us how to be present to reality, to the mystery of life. He was teaching us how to receive reality before we judge and categorise it, and fit it into our own existing point of view. Just as our eyes become accustomed gradually to a darkened room, he was teaching us that if we can accept emptiness then we will slowly learn to experience it as fullness. This lies at the heart of the contemplative gaze as we learn how to see fully and be present. Many find this too difficult and too challenging and give up silent prayer, which seems to be a waste of time to the rational mind.

In a limited sense, they are correct: for our western time-bound mentality, silent prayer is precisely a waste of time. It is not productive, it doesn't seem to achieve anything. As I sit there, my ego reminds me of all the important things I could be doing. This is a real crisis in any commitment to silent prayer. If we can remain faithful to the practice we begin to unlearn rather than learn.

What we unlearn first is how much our spirituality and our whole way of life is dominated by wilfulness and will-power. Our time-bound culture has an inbuilt restlessness, and this kind of drive has created so many wonderful technical achievements in our age. We are *can-do* people. This is fine in terms of material success, but in the spiritual life it is counter-productive. Too many religious believers are convinced that there has to be some special technique by which I can run my spiritual life. Generally speaking, in the Christian west this is understood to be in the area of morality. Most people thing that is what religion is all about. Give me some rules and some commandments to obey, some rituals to follow, some words to say and I can achieve my salvation. We like to push reality and to control it. As I said earlier, this even creeps into my prayer life which is reduced to saying prayers to get God to do something for me. If he doesn't seem to answer my immediate request at least the prayer will go into my credit account and help me to save my soul.

Contemplative prayer teaches me that I don't have to attain anything because I already have everything. Contemplative prayer is concerned with the mystery of Being rather than my programme for doing. Many years ago Blessed Duns Scotus taught that all Being is one. God is Pure Being, the Great I Am, and we all participate in the gift of Being. This applies to the whole of creation and was called the Great Chain of Being. Western technology lost this connection. We became rather arrogant and thought we could rule the world. We split ourselves off from the essential unity of everything that exists. The present moment was never anything special or worthy of much attention because we were busy creating a better future.

Thankfully our scientists today are rediscovering the sense of mystery at the heart of everything. Einstein spoke of his profound humility before the unknowable mysteries of the universe. They speak about the mysterious energy at the heart of everything created. Everything is connected in a flow of movement and relationship. We are surrounded by a cosmic benevolence. We are learning that time and space are relative.

> Space and time – constructs of our mind – implode in the mystery of the now. The word presence (with spatial and temporal overtones) invites us into the depth realization of this.[72]

We are learning again now, with some humility, to be truly present, to be present to the now. We are learning to move from controlling reality, to surrendering to it. What does this mean?

---

[72] Barbara Fiand *Awe-Filled Wonder* (Paulist Press International U S) p 58

In Christian language, we are recovering the traditional teaching of the sacrament of the present moment. In contemplative prayer we learn to sit in silence and in stillness, to go into what Jesus called our inner room. As we sit, attentive to our breathing, our awareness of this moment opens us to that which transcends this moment. Our awareness of this breath makes us conscious of the God from whom every breath comes. The experience of silence moves us into the silence that is the Word of God. Our experience of emptiness allows us to receive the fullness that is the grace and love of God. Here again, it is interesting to note how scientists are speaking like the mystics, as they try to describe the mysterious emptiness in which everything exists. Brian Swimme speaks of an *empty fullness*. The mystics speak not so much of knowing but *tasting* reality and feeling the depths of an intelligent mystery that enfolds everything, in which everything arises, dies and then is transformed into something new.

The Christian mystery of the Trinity describes this constant flow of life and love, of mutual giving and receiving. For us this mystery of Being becomes personal and explains our deepest need and desire for someone to love, to surrender to. We can never fully taste such love in this life but we feel it in the desires and longings of the human heart. We long for presence. The playwright Samuel Beckett expresses this in *Waiting for Godot*. Two tramps sit by a stunted tree waiting to be met, to be seen, to be noticed. When a passing boy tells them Godot is not coming, Vladimir cries out, *Tell him you saw me…that you saw me*. The words are used at the end of every act. We long to be noticed.

Moving from religion as morality, to religion as mysticism, we discover that it is all about presence. Religion is not about *effort* but *consent*. Effort keeps the ego in charge; consent surrenders to the presence of mystery. We cannot make it happen by our will-power. We allow it to happen through our willingness, which is another word for obedience to reality. Gradually as we go about our daily routines we will experience moments when the transcendent becomes visible. We will begin to look upon people with compassion and love rather than judgement. We will see it in the face of a child, or a mother caring for her children, we will see it in the old and the not so beautiful. We will experience it, especially in the presence of a friend and even in the presence of an enemy. It may not be the same intensity for both, but to be awakened to the presence of God in someone I usually see as a threat is an enormous grace, one that could save our world. We are beginning to learn that each moment offers this gift of Being to us. Each moment hints at the deeper mystery of The Being that contains everything.

Becoming present also teaches us how to embrace the limitations of this present moment. This is the great gift of the incarnation: when Christ emptied himself of his glory to transform this particular *moment*, this particular *now*, with all its limitations, into the glow of his divinity. We begin to overcome the duality of things. In silent prayer, we don't need to *push the river*; we discover that we are in it. Looking at the setting sun, we merge with the reality of the sun while remaining distinct from it. We sense the unified reality of everything that exists. In the same way, when we pray silently we touch the depths of our souls, where the Holy Spirit lives and pulls us into the flow of love between Christ and the Father. We discover the meaning of the words at the end of the Eucharistic prayer: *through him, with him, in him*. Our little, finite selves are a microcosm of what God is doing in every aspect of creation. We are a part of the great mystery of a loving evolutionary process that includes the greatest coincidence of opposites, the pattern of life and death, in which everything can be transformed through the power of Christ's Resurrection.

Biblical spirituality reminds us that we need to move out of our time-bound *business-as-usual* stance. That was the purpose of the Sabbath: to remind the Jewish people of the need to balance doing with being, of the need to become truly present to reality. Sadly it became all too legalised, but it was meant to break the addiction to our obsession with doing. It was a brilliant attempt to get people off the conveyor belt of their lives and become present to the eternal now; to break the bonds of time by seeing eternity breaking through in the present moment. We have seen that the mind cannot really access the present. The only way to access the present is to be present. The mind just wants to *think* things.

We learn to surrender to the loving mystery at the heart of all things when we realise, as St Symeon, the new theologian, reminds us, that God dwells within each one of us. This is the ancient wisdom that we had almost lost in recent centuries. The Incarnation is the foundational sign that this is true. It is the supreme icon of presence. Christ is the one who puts it all together, where eternity meets time and declares that it is all one. Timeless eternity in the Godhead becomes this particular human being, Jesus of Nazareth, in a particular time and a particular culture. It is not surprising that non-Christian religions, atheists and others find the idea too shocking to accept. I think many of us Christians find it difficult to embrace it fully. We just want to keep creating divisions and boundaries between spirit and matter. We fight to keep our dualisms in place, while always placing ourselves, and our own belonging group on the right side of the fence.

Eventually, like Jacob, we stop fighting God and learn to accept our woundedness. Acceptance of who we are with our own particular form of weakness and imperfection is not an obstacle to God but the very thing that draws God to us. We move out of our mind-games of trying fruitlessly to work everything out, into the spaciousness of the heart. This is not about sentiment or feeling. Contemplative prayer takes us to a deeper level than feeling. It is a much more subtle awareness of loving attention which can exist even in the absence of emotion. Jesus tried, in his teaching, to move us beyond emotional attachment to a deeper place. When the people are first attracted to him they look for signs and wonders. Jesus says that the only sign he will give them is that of the prophet Jonah. It is his metaphor for the great mystery of death being transformed into new life. The emotional programmes of *the false self* have to die.

Our sense of separate, independent existence, therefore, has to die. Then we can become present to the new life which is always available twenty-four hours a day. It is the mystery of Being which contains everything. Ken Wilbur tells us that we live in a universe of holons. A holon includes all parts. The mystics tell us that if we can get our judging mind out of the way we can see the mystery of Being in every object. The secret is to receive it as it is, not to try to fit it into our mindset. We see it in a leaf or a flower, hear it in the song of a bird, arising out of nothing. We ourselves have been created out of nothing to enjoy this wonderful mystery of conscious Being. The religion of morals, dogmas and rituals only exists to lead us to become present to this loving mystery. This is the one thing necessary as Jesus tells us, *the pearl of great price, the treasure hidden in the field*.

The structure of religious faith is there to lead us further into this mystery, given to us at our Baptism. We already have everything that we need. The flow of life and energy in the universe is in our deepest DNA, which is God. *My deepest me is God* says Catherine of Genoa. Jesus took on our human nature so that he could transform us into divinity. This is the great mystery of transformation. We don't get there by our willpower, by fighting to overcome our faults. We get there by surrendering to the reality that *God is loving God in us,* and that includes our imperfection and woundedness.

The Risen Christ carries the wounds that we have given him as marks of glory. This glory is the mystery of forgiveness and compassion that flows into our hearts every moment of every day. The key to the mystery is allowing God to love us. Contemplative prayer takes us to the deepest part of our being, where this can happen by the power of the Spirit. Here the gifts of our Baptism are activated, often at a deeper level than we can know. We find that, almost without trying, we become more compassionate people in every-day life. We find it almost impossible to hate anyone else, because we have learned the hardest lesson of all: that the presence of God means that we no longer have to hate ourselves. All is one, all is connected to the flow of life and love that is the pure Being of God.

Mature spirituality calls for the deepest humility. An acceptance of precisely who I am in God, that I do not have to become worthy of this kind of love. Nothing I have ever done in the past can ever get in the way of that. The future belongs to God. The only time Jesus speaks about the future is to tell us not to worry about it. For too long we Christians have pushed everything into the future. Will I get to heaven? Will I save my soul? We forget to enjoy the only moment we have which is the now. In Jesus we see the eternal now breaking into our ordinary time. This gives a sacred dimension to everything that we can see and hear. We learn not so much to rush into saving the world, but just to look, to enjoy, to see the beauty, to taste the presence. This is what all the mystics call, *living in the Eternal now*. This is why Thomas Merton can say, *The Gate of Heaven is everywhere*. This is living in the kingdom. This is what Jesus means when he says that *eternal life is now*. Then our action on behalf of others will come from our true centre. It will not be so much my action, as God working through me.

We can glimpse what Jesus means when he says that the poor possess the kingdom. Material things are not bad, but we tend to cling to them for significance and meaning. They shore up the private self. The poor have to find meaning somewhere else. By becoming detached from possessing and clinging, we begin to truly possess things. We learn to really see them in their depth and beauty as they really are. Everything in creation then opens up for the truly poor, non-possessing person. This is what Jesus meant when he told the disciples of John the Baptist that the poor were hearing good news, that they could see and hear reality in a new non-judging way.

All we have to do is to receive the gift of the kingdom, by becoming present to the mystery of love both within and without. St John of the Cross says that at the end of our lives we will be examined in love. Whenever we are fully present we are in love, and whatever we become fully present to in love will never be lost. It will survive death, because it is already participating in the eternal now.

Conclusion

The situation of the soul in contemplation is
something like the situation of Adam and Eve in
Paradise. Everything is yours, but on one infinitely
important condition: that it is all *given*. There is
nothing that you can claim, nothing that you can
demand, nothing that you can *take*. And as soon as
you try to take something as if it were your own –
you lose your Eden.[73]

[73] Thomas Merton *New Seeds of Contemplation* (New Directions Paperback 1972) p 229

Thomas Merton was very fond of William Faulkner's short story, *The Bear*. It describes the coming of age of Ike McCaslin, a young boy who wanted to become a hunter. He had long been fascinated by the tales of older men about a bear named Old Ben. Very few had ever seen it. Ike decided that whatever it would take, he would find this bear.

Early one morning he left the safety of his home for the forest armed with his gun, a watch and a compass. The gun would protect him from attack, the watch would tell him the time in the dense forest, and the compass would provide him with his sense of direction. After some time he finds footprints and becomes aware that although he cannot see the bear he senses that it is watching him. Reaching a clearing he makes a major decision. He puts down his gun, his watch and his compass; he sits down on a log and simply waits.

After some time Old Ben appears before him. The bear looks at him and moves on. Over the next four years he sees the bear on two other occasions. Even though he has his gun with him, he *fails* to kill the bear.

Thomas Merton suggested that the hunter is a symbol of someone searching for God. It is fascinating to see this story as a model for contemplative prayer. It is only when Ike divests himself of his gun, compass and watch that he is able to see the bear. The gun symbolises the defences of *the false self* and the egocentric mind. It is only when we can drop our defences, our fixing and pigeon-holing judgements that we can be open to seeing reality as it truly is. As long as we allow ourselves to live at lower levels of consciousness, we will not be open to the mystery of *the Other*. We will just fit everything into our own limited mindset. We have to put that *gun* down to truly meet reality.

The watch represents our clinging to the time as past and future. Whenever we sit in silent prayer, our calculating minds either take us back into the past to revisit old wounds and memories, or project us into the future of plans and projects. What we miss is the now, the only moment we have. Contemplation allows the breaking-in of the eternal now into ordinary time. We learn to see what is before us without approval or disapproval. It is as it is.

The Greeks had two words for time: *kronos* and *kairos*. *Kronos* refers to chronological time, or business as usual. This is ordinary time in which we try to predict, control and measure what is happening to us. *Kairos* time is the breaking in of the eternal now. It is what the gospels call the fullness of time. At such a moment Jesus breaks into our world in the mystery of incarnation. We live our lives between *kronos* and *kairos*, between the *now* of the kingdom and the *not yet*. Some live without any awareness of *kairos* time – *When did we see you, Lord?* Others experience it in nature, or through art, literature, in the theatre, or watching a good film. The *now* is the moment of union, of recognition, of joy, of presence to the mystery. It is an experience of the depth present in all things.

If *kairos* time is the *now*, *kronos* time is *the not yet*. *The not yet* is the reminder that the kingdom is not fully realised. It therefore propels us into our work for justice, as we struggle to create a better world. We need both experiences of time, because unless we experience moments of presence and union, our work for others is not rooted in true compassion. We can easily resort to either/or, black or white judgements. We seek to punish rather than heal. The ego always splits into dualistic judgements recognising the kingdom here but not there. Moments of *kairos* time teach us to take on the mind of Christ. We become inclusive not exclusive, even of our enemies. We learn to see God's transformative presence in everything, even in the darkest situations. In *kairos* time we learn to see.

The compass represents our strong desire to control our lives, to know where we are heading. The dark forest is a powerful symbol of the dark night of the soul. Many people give up contemplative prayer because they cannot measure any progress. They feel lost, but, like the young Ike McCaslin, we have to put the compass down and trust the experience of waiting, of surrendering our security systems and our plans. Ike didn't find the bear; he was granted a sight, while he was sitting, waiting, doing nothing. He had learned how to become present to mystery. His initiation wasn't based on killing a prey. He had been taught a deep reverence and respect for the mystery of Being.

The most difficult challenge for the spiritual seeker is to accept failure. Over the years we learn that despite all our efforts we can never shake off our faults and failings. This is the part of us that has to die, and it is painful. We much prefer observing commandments, going to Mass, saying prayers, believing in doctrines, to the surrender of our wounded hearts to God by trusting a mystery that we cannot control. The great discovery is that we do not have to find God, we have already been found by God. God is present in the very core of our being. This presence offers total acceptance, total forgiveness, unconditional love.

Some of the mystics speak about the importance of the gift of tears. What they are saying is that God always loves us and embraces us especially in our weakness and woundedness. This is the constant teaching of Jesus about his forgiving Father and the forgiving gift of the Spirit which he breathed into his apostles. It was expressed in his own moment of excruciating pain and humiliation on the Cross when he summed up his whole life in the words, *Father forgive them, they do not know what they are doing.* To know God at any depth is to experience forgiveness.

Silent prayer invites us to a place where we can learn and look, with the compassion of God, at everything we see. This is the gift of tears and those tears need to be expressed first for ourselves, as we sit with our poverty and emptiness before God, our repeated failures and our wounds. Gradually, we discover that there is no place within the forest of our hearts where God cannot be present to embrace and to forgive. We then look with compassionate eyes and hearts at everything we see and meet. This is wholeness. This is transformation. As Jesus says, *If your eye is sound your whole body is sound.* The wounds are always the way in. Just let your heart pray.

Other books by Michael J Cunningham SDB

Within and Without
Renewing Religious Life (2003)

A Time for Compassion
Spirituality for Today (2005)

Lost & Found
Spirituality for a Changing World (2007)

Other Don Bosco Publications

Don't Organise My Tears *Reflections On Bereavement* A Bailey

School Ethos & Chaplaincy D O'Malley

Christian Leadership In Education D O'Malley

The Christian Teacher D O'Malley

Ordinary Ways *Spiritual Reflections For Teachers & Youth Leaders* D O'Malley

Prayers To Close The Day D O'Malley

Prayers To Start The Day D O'Malley

Trust The Road *2nd Edition With Coloured Illustrations* D O'Malley

Via Lucis *How To Pray The Stations Of The Resurrection* D O'Malley

Serving The Young *Our Catholic Schools Today* J Gallagher

101 Saints And Special People *Lives Of Saints For Children* K Pearce

Chloe And Jack Visit The Vatican *A Child's Guide To The Vatican* K Pearce

St John Bosco *The Friend Of Children And Young People* K Pearce

Good News In The Family *The Life Of Jesus In Story Form* K Pearce

Memory Game *Based On '101 Saints And Special People'* K Pearce

Our Colourful Church Year *A Child's Guide To The Church Year* K Pearce

Rosie And Katie Go To Mass *A Child's Guide To The Mass* K Pearce

Rosie Goes To Church (Book & DVD) *A Child's Guide To The Church* K Pearce

Sean Devereux *A Life Given For Africa 1964-1993* M Delmer

God Of Many Faces *Reflective Verses* M Renshaw

Don Bosco's Gospel Way *Reflections On The Life Of Don Bosco* M Winstanley

Moving On *Book Of Reflective Poetry* M J Cooke

Mamma Margaret *The Life Of Don Bosco's Mother* T Bosco

Teacher, Teach Us To Pray *For Use In Primary Schools* W Acred

The Witnesses *Seven Witnesses Narrate Their Part In The Passion* W Acred